Dreamweaver CS4
Basic

Student Manual

ACE Edition

Dreamweaver CS4 Basic

President & Chief Executive Officer:	Jon Winder
Vice President, Product Development:	Matt Gambino
Vice President, Operations:	Josh Pincus
Director of Publishing Systems Development:	Dan Quackenbush
Developmental Editor:	Brandon Heffernan
Copyeditor:	Catherine Oliver
Keytester:	Clifford Coryea

Trademarks

ILT Series is a trademark of Axzo Press.

Some of the product names and company names used in this book have been used for identification purposes only and may be trademarks or registered trademarks of their respective manufacturers and sellers.

Disclaimers

We reserve the right to revise this publication and make changes from time to time in its content without notice.

The Adobe Approved Certification Courseware logo is either a registered trademark or trademark of Adobe Systems Incorporated in the United States and/or other countries. The Adobe Approved Certification Courseware logo is a proprietary trademark of Adobe. All rights reserved.

The ILT Series is independent from ProCert Labs, LLC and Adobe Systems Incorporated, and are not affiliated with ProCert Labs and Adobe in any manner. This publication may assist students to prepare for an Adobe Certified Expert exam, however, neither ProCert Labs nor Adobe warrant that use of this material will ensure success in connection with any exam.

ISBN 10: 1-4260-0498-2
ISBN 13: 978-1-4260-0498-8

Student Manual with data CD
ISBN-10: 1-4260-0500-8
ISBN-13: 978-1-4260-0500-8

Printed in the United States of America

1 2 3 4 5 6 7 8 9 10 GL 11 10 09

Contents

Introduction

After reading this introduction, you'll know how to:

A Use ILT Series manuals in general.

B Use prerequisites, a target student description, course objectives, and a skills inventory to properly set your expectations for the course.

C Re-key this course after class.

Topic A: About the manual

ILT Series philosophy

Our manuals facilitate your learning by providing structured interaction with the software itself. While we provide text to explain difficult concepts, the hands-on activities are the focus of our courses. By paying close attention as your instructor leads you through these activities, you'll learn the skills and concepts effectively.

We believe strongly in the instructor-led class. During class, focus on your instructor. Our manuals are designed and written to facilitate your interaction with your instructor and not to call attention to manuals themselves.

We believe in the basic approach of setting expectations, delivering instruction, and providing summary and review afterwards. For this reason, lessons begin with objectives and end with summaries. We also provide overall course objectives and a course summary to provide both an introduction to and closure on the entire course.

Manual components

The manuals contain these major components:

- Table of contents
- Introduction
- Units
- Appendix
- Course summary
- Quick reference
- Glossary
- Index

Each element is described below.

Table of contents

The table of contents acts as a learning roadmap.

Introduction

The introduction contains information about our training philosophy and our manual components, features, and conventions. It contains target student, prerequisite, objective, and setup information for the specific course.

Units

Units are the largest structural component of the course content. A unit begins with a title page that lists objectives for each major subdivision, or topic, within the unit. Within each topic, conceptual and explanatory information alternates with hands-on activities. Units conclude with a summary comprising one paragraph for each topic, and an independent practice activity that gives you an opportunity to practice the skills you've learned.

The conceptual information takes the form of text paragraphs, exhibits, lists, and tables. The activities are structured in two columns, one telling you what to do, the other providing explanations, descriptions, and graphics.

Appendix

The appendix for this course lists the Adobe Certified Expert (ACE) exam objectives for Dreamweaver CS4, along with references to corresponding coverage in ILT Series courseware.

Course summary

This section provides a text summary of the entire course. It's useful for providing closure at the end of the course. The course summary also indicates the next course in this series, if there is one, and lists additional resources you might find useful as you continue to learn about the software.

Quick reference

The quick reference is an at-a-glance job aid summarizing some of the more common features of the software.

Glossary

The glossary provides definitions for all of the key terms used in this course.

Index

The index at the end of this manual makes it easy for you to find information about a particular software component, feature, or concept.

Manual conventions

We've tried to keep the number of elements and the types of formatting to a minimum in the manuals. This approach aids in clarity and makes the manuals more elegant looking. But there are some conventions and icons you should know about.

Item	Description
Italic text	In conceptual text, indicates a new term or feature.
Bold text	In unit summaries, indicates a key term or concept. In an independent practice activity, indicates an explicit item that you select, choose, or type.
`Code font`	Indicates code or syntax.
`Longer strings of ▶ code will look ▶ like this.`	In the hands-on activities, any code that's too long to fit on a single line is divided into segments by one or more continuation characters (▶). This code should be entered as a continuous string of text.
Select **bold item**	In the left column of hands-on activities, bold sans-serif text indicates an explicit item that you select, choose, or type.
Keycaps like (↵ ENTER)	Indicate a key on the keyboard you must press.

Hands-on activities

The hands-on activities are the most important parts of our manuals. They're divided into two primary columns. The "Here's how" column gives short instructions to you about what to do. The "Here's why" column provides explanations, graphics, and clarifications. Here's a sample:

Do it!

A-1: Creating a commission formula

Here's how	Here's why
1 Open Sales	This is an oversimplified sales compensation worksheet. It shows sales totals, commissions, and incentives for five sales reps.
2 Observe the contents of cell F4	F4 ▼ = =E4*C_Rate The commission rate formulas use the name "C_Rate" instead of a value for the commission rate.

For these activities, we've provided a collection of data files designed to help you learn each skill in a real-world business context. As you work through the activities, you modify and update these files. Of course, you might make a mistake and therefore want to re-key the activity starting from scratch. To make it easy to start over, you rename each data file at the end of the first activity in which the file is modified. Our convention for renaming files is to add the word "My" to the beginning of the file name. In the above activity, for example, a file called "Sales" is being used for the first time. At the end of this activity, you would save the file as "My sales," thus leaving the "Sales" file unchanged. If you make a mistake, you can start over using the original "Sales" file.

In some activities, however, it might not be practical to rename the data file. If you want to retry one of these activities, ask your instructor for a fresh copy of the original data file.

Topic B: Setting your expectations

Properly setting your expectations is essential to your success. This topic will help you do that by providing:

- Prerequisites for this course
- A description of the target student
- A list of the objectives for the course
- A skills assessment for the course

Course prerequisites

Before taking this course, you should be familiar with personal computers and the use of a keyboard and a mouse. Furthermore, this course assumes that you've completed the following courses or have equivalent experience:

- *Windows XP: Basic* or *Windows Vista: Basic*

Target student

This course will benefit students who want to learn how to use Dreamweaver CS4 to create and modify Web sites. You'll learn how to plan, define, and create a Web site; add pages and content; format text; create and apply CSS style rules; create links and tables; manage images and other files; and publish a site. You should be comfortable using a PC and have experience with Microsoft Windows XP or Vista. You should have little or no experience with Dreamweaver.

Adobe ACE certification

This course is designed to help you pass the Adobe Certified Expert (ACE) exam for Dreamweaver CS4. For complete certification training, you should complete this course and *Dreamweaver CS4: Advanced, ACE Edition*.

Course objectives

These overall course objectives will give you an idea about what to expect from the course. It's also possible that they'll help you see that this course isn't the right one for you. If you think you either lack the prerequisite knowledge or already know most of the subject matter to be covered, you should let your instructor know that you think you're misplaced in the class.

Note: In addition the general objectives listed below, specific ACE exam objectives are listed at the beginning of each topic (where applicable). For a complete mapping of ACE objectives to ILT Series content, see Appendix A.

After completing this course, you'll know how to:

- Discuss basic Internet and HTML concepts, identify the components of the Dreamweaver CS4 workspace, create a custom workspace, edit and format text, insert images, preview pages in a browser, identify basic HTML tags, and perform basic tasks in Code view.

- Plan and define a Web site, work with the Files panel and the Assets panel, create a Web page, import text from external files, set basic page properties, and use Find and Replace to update content and code.

- Define a basic page structure, create and modify lists, create CSS style sheets, apply styles to text, and create class styles.

- Create tables and nested tables, format rows and cells, merge cells, add rows and columns, set fixed and variable widths for tables and columns, and change cell borders and padding.

- Create links to other pages and resources, create named anchors and link to them, create e-mail links, create image maps, and apply CSS styles to link states.

- Choose appropriate image formats, write effective alternate text, modify image properties, and insert and modify background images.

- Check file size and download times, check for broken links and orphaned files, cloak files, validate code, connect to a Web server, and upload and update a site.

Skills inventory

Use the following form to gauge your skill level entering the class. For each skill listed, rate your familiarity from 1 to 5, with five being the most familiar. *This isn't a test*. Rather, it's intended to provide you with an idea of where you're starting from at the beginning of class. If you're wholly unfamiliar with all the skills, you might not be ready for the class. If you think you already understand all of the skills, you might need to move on to the next course in the series. In either case, you should let your instructor know as soon as possible.

Skill	1	2	3	4	5
Identifying components of the Dreamweaver workspace					
Creating a custom workspace					
Inserting, editing, and formatting text					
Inserting images					
Previewing pages in a browser					
Working with the code tools					
Defining a site					
Creating and titling Web pages					
Importing text					
Setting page properties					
Inserting special characters and spaces					
Using Find and Replace to update content					
Defining a page structure					
Creating and modifying lists					
Creating and attaching external style sheets					
Defining element styles with CSS					
Creating and applying class styles					
Creating tables and nested tables					
Adding and formatting rows, columns, and individual cells					
Setting fixed and variable table widths					
Creating links to other pages and resources					
Creating named anchors and linking to them					

Skill	1	2	3	4	5
Creating e-mail links					
Creating image maps					
Applying CSS styles to link states					
Choosing appropriate image formats					
Writing effective alternate text					
Modifying image properties					
Inserting and modifying background images					
Checking file size and download times					
Fixing broken links					
Locating orphaned files					
Cloaking files and folders					
Validating code					
Connecting to a remote server					
Uploading and updating a site					

Topic C: Re-keying the course

If you have the proper hardware and software, you can re-key this course after class. This section explains what you'll need in order to do so and how to do it.

Hardware requirements

Your personal computer should have:

- A keyboard and a mouse
- Intel® Pentium® 4 or equivalent processor
- 512 MB RAM
- 1 GB of hard-disk space
- A DVD-ROM drive for installation
- A monitor set to a minimum resolution of 1280 x 960 and 24-bit color or better. (Users of LCD or widescreen displays should choose the monitor's native resolution, if possible.)

Software requirements

You also need the following software:

- Microsoft® Windows® XP with Service Pack 2, or Windows Vista™ Home Premium, Business, Ultimate, or Enterprise (certified for 32-bit editions), updated with the most recent service packs
- Dreamweaver CS4
- Microsoft Outlook, Thunderbird, or another e-mail client (required to complete Activity A-3 in the "Links" unit)
- Microsoft Word 2000, XP, 2003, or 2007 (required to complete Activity B-2 in the "Web sites and pages" unit)

Network requirements

The following network components and connectivity are also required for re-keying this course:

- Internet access, for the following purposes:
  - Updating the Windows operating system at update.microsoft.com.
  - Completing Activity A-3 in the "Links" unit
  - Downloading the Student Data files (if necessary)

Setup instructions to re-key the course

Before you re-key the course, you need to perform the following steps.

1 Install Windows XP Professional on an NTFS partition according to the software manufacturer's instructions.

   Note: You can also use Windows Vista, but the screen shots in this course were taken in Windows XP, so your screens might look somewhat different.

2 If the operating system is Windows XP, then launch the Control Panel, open the Display Properties dialog box and apply the following settings:

   • Theme—Windows XP

   • Screen resolution—1280 by 960 pixels

   • Color quality—High (24 bit) or higher

   Note: To avoid a blurred or distorted screen, users of flat panel or widescreen displays should either choose the monitor's native resolution, or disable image stretching and scaling, if possible.

3 If Windows was already loaded on this PC, verify that Internet Explorer is the default Web browser. (If you installed Windows yourself, skip this step.)

   a Click Start and choose All Programs, Internet Explorer.

   b Choose Tools, Internet Options.

   c Check "Internet Explorer should check to see whether it is the default browser."

   d Click OK to close the Internet Options dialog box.

   e Close and re-open Internet Explorer.

   f If a prompt appears, asking you to make Internet Explorer your default browser, click Yes.

   g Close Internet Explorer.

4 Connect to the Internet.

5 Open Internet Explorer and navigate to update.microsoft.com. Update the operating system with the latest critical updates and service packs.

6 Install Dreamweaver CS4 according to the software manufacturer's instructions.

7 Install Microsoft Outlook, Thunderbird, or any similar e-mail application. Accept all defaults during installation. (This action is required to complete Activity A-3 in the "Links" unit.)

8 Install Microsoft Word 2000, XP, 2003, or 2007 according to the software manufacturer's instructions. Accept all defaults during installation. (This is required to complete Activity B-2 in the "Web sites and pages" unit.)

9 If necessary, reset any defaults that you've changed. If you don't wish to reset the defaults, you can still re-key the course, but some activities might not work exactly as documented.

10 Adjust the computer's display settings as follows:

   a Right-click the desktop and choose Properties to open the Display Properties dialog box.

   b On the Settings tab, change the Color quality to 16 bit or higher, and change the Screen resolution to 1024 by 768 pixels. (If your monitor is small, consider using a higher screen resolution, if possible.)

   c On the Appearance tab, set Windows and buttons to Windows XP style.

   d Click OK. If you're prompted to accept the new settings, click OK and click Yes. Then, if necessary, close the Display Properties dialog box.

11 Change Internet properties as follows:

   a Start Internet Explorer. Choose Tools, Internet Options.

   b On the General tab, click Use Blank and click Apply.

   c On the Advanced tab, under Security, check "Allow active content to run in files on My Computer" and click Apply. (This option appears only if you updated Windows XP with Service Pack 2.)

   d Close the Internet Options dialog box, and close Internet Explorer.

12 If necessary, create an e-mail account in your e-mail client. (You don't actually send or receive messages in this course, so a fully functional e-mail account isn't needed. Without an e-mail client, you can't complete activity A-3 in the Links unit.)

13 Display file extensions.

   a Start Windows Explorer.

   b Choose Tools, Folder Options and select the View tab.

   c Clear the check box for "Hide extensions for known file types."

   d Close Windows Explorer.

14 Create a folder called Student Data at the root of the hard drive (C:\).

15 Download the Student Data files for the course. (If you don't have an Internet connection, you can ask your instructor for a copy of the data files on a disk.)

   a Connect to www.axzopress.com.

   b Under Downloads, click Instructor-Led Training.

   c Browse the subject categories to locate your course. Then click the course title to display a list of available downloads. (You can also access these downloads through our Catalog listings.)

   d Click the link(s) for downloading the Student Data files, and follow the instructions that appear on your screen.

16 Copy the data files to the Student Data folder.

CertBlaster exam preparation for ACE certification

CertBlaster pre- and post-assessment software is available for this course. To download and install this free software, complete the following steps:

1   Go to www.axzopress.com.

2   Under Downloads, click CertBlaster.

3   Click the link for Dreamweaver CS4.

4   Save the .EXE file to a folder on your hard drive. (**Note:** If you skip this step, the CertBlaster software will not install correctly.)

5   Click Start and choose Run.

6   Click Browse and navigate to the folder that contains the .EXE file.

7   Select the .EXE file and click Open.

8   Click OK and follow the on-screen instructions. When prompted for the password, enter **c_dwCS4**.

Unit 1

Getting started

Unit time: 60 minutes

Complete this unit, and you'll know how to:

A Discuss basic Internet, HTML, and XHTML concepts.

B Identify components of the Dreamweaver CS4 workspace, and create a custom workspace.

C Insert and edit text, insert images, and preview a page in a browser.

D Switch between document views, identify basic HTML tags, perform basic tasks in Code view, and use the tag selector and the Quick Tag Editor.

Topic A: Internet basics

Explanation

Before you start using Dreamweaver CS4 to design and create Web sites, you should first understand the basics of the Internet, the Web, and HTML.

The Internet and the Web

The *Internet* is a vast array of networks that belong to universities, businesses, organizations, governments, and individuals all over the world. The World Wide Web, or simply the *Web*, is one of many services of the Internet. Other Internet services include e-mail, File Transfer Protocol (FTP), and instant messaging.

To view Web pages and other content, you need a Web browser, such as Internet Explorer, Firefox, or Safari. Web content typically includes text, images, and multimedia files. Each page or resource has a unique address known as a *Uniform Resource Locater* (URL).

A *Web site* is a collection of linked pages. The top-level page is commonly called the *home page*. A home page typically provides hyperlinks to navigate to other pages within the site or to external pages. A *hyperlink*—or more commonly, a *link*—is text or an image that, when clicked, takes the user to another page, another location on the current page, another Web site, or a specific file.

HTML

Hypertext Markup Language, or *HTML,* is a standard markup language on the Web. HTML enables you to structure and present your Web site's content. An HTML document is a plain text file that contains HTML code, along with the content for a Web page. Exhibit 1-1 shows an example of a simple HTML document. HTML documents have an .htm or .html file extension.

HTML code encloses your text content and defines the basic structure of a Web page. A Web page can contain links, images, multimedia files, and other elements. When a browser opens a Web page, the text typically loads quickly, while images and embedded media files might take longer.

XHTML

Extensible Hypertext Markup Language, or XHTML, is a more efficient and strict version of HTML. For years, browser makers introduced proprietary tags and attributes in an effort to give Web designers more control over the look and feel of their Web pages. Unfortunately, most of these elements and attributes served only to make Web page code bloated, cluttered, and semantically meaningless. Because XHTML doesn't allow proprietary tags or attributes, the result is cleaner, more efficient code that is more evenly supported across different browsers. Dreamweaver CS4 builds Web pages with XHTML code by default.

```
<!DOCTYPE html PUBLIC "-//W3C//DTD XHTML 1.0 Transitional//EN" "http://
<html xmlns="http://www.w3.org/1999/xhtml">
<head>
<meta http-equiv="Content-Type" content="text/html; charset=utf-8" />
<title>Chili Facts</title>
</head>

<body>
<h1>Chilis</h1>
<p>Chilis add zest to many recipes. </p>
<img src="chilis.jpg" alt="Chilis" />
</body>
</html>
```

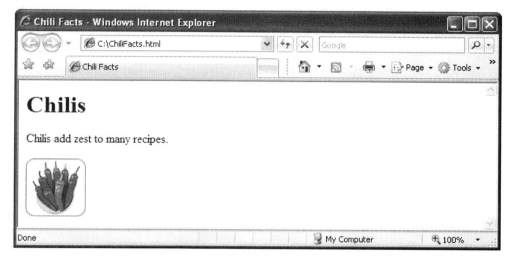

Exhibit 1-1: A simple Web page shown as XHTML code and in a browser

Do it! **A-1: Discussing the Web, HTML, and XHTML**

Questions and answers
1 What's the difference between the Internet and the World Wide Web?
2 What other Internet services are there?
3 What's a Web page?
4 What's a Web site?
5 What's a Web browser?
6 What's HTML?
7 What's XHTML?

Topic B: The Dreamweaver CS4 workspace

This topic covers the following Adobe ACE exam objectives for Dreamweaver CS4.

#	Objective
2.2	Locate files associated with a Dreamweaver site.
2.3	Manage files associated with a Dreamweaver site.
4.3	Given a visual aid, explain the purpose of and/or when to use that visual aid.
4.4	Work with the Properties panel and Tag Editor.
5.3	Explain how to get information about tags.

Web authoring in Dreamweaver CS4

Explanation

Dreamweaver CS4 is Web authoring software that helps you design and create Web sites and applications. When you create or change a page in the Dreamweaver workspace, Dreamweaver automatically generates the required XHTML, CSS, or scripting code for the page. You can also write or edit code manually. Before you get started creating Web sites, you should become familiar with the Dreamweaver CS4 workspace.

Starting Dreamweaver and opening a file

When you start Dreamweaver CS4 for the first time, the Default Editor dialog box opens, prompting you to verify that you want to use Dreamweaver as the default editor for several types of files. Click OK, or change the default selections as needed. The welcome screen appears, as shown in Exhibit 1-2. If you don't want the welcome screen to appear the next time you start Dreamweaver, check "Don't show again" (at the bottom of the screen), and click OK. A new, blank HTML page opens in Split view, which is a combination of Design view and Code view. You can start building with this default HTML page, or you can close it and open another file.

To open an existing file, choose File, Open and browse to locate the file you want to open. Select the file and click Open, or double-click the file.

To start a new file, choose File, New. The New Document dialog box opens, and by default, the blank HTML page option is selected. Click Create to start a new HTML page.

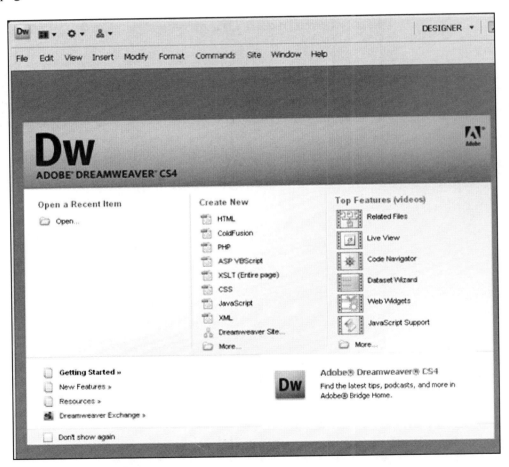

Exhibit 1-2: The welcome screen

Interface components

As shown in Exhibit 1-3, the default Dreamweaver CS4 interface components include the Document toolbar, the document window, the Insert panel, the Files panel, and the Properties panel.

Properties panel   Document toolbar   Document window   Insert panel   Files panel
(Split view)

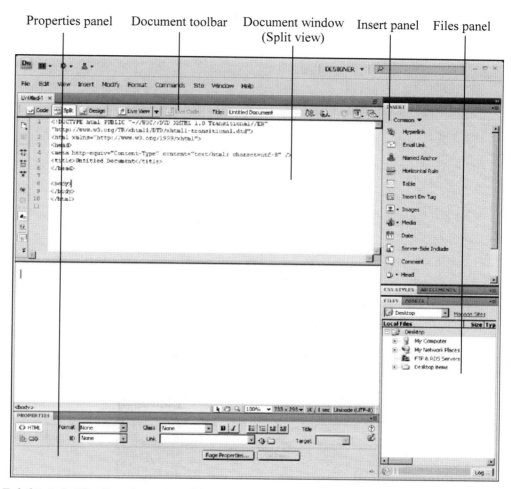

Exhibit 1-3: The Dreamweaver CS4 interface

The following table describes the components of the Dreamweaver CS4 interface.

Component	Description
Insert panel	Provides buttons you can use to quickly insert elements such as images, tables, and `<div>` tags into a document.
Document toolbar	Provides buttons you can use to perform a variety of common tasks. For example, you can switch between Code view, Design view, and Split view, and you can upload files, check for errors, and preview a page in a Web browser.
Document window	Displays the current Web page.
Files panel	Displays your site folders and files. You can open a file by double-clicking it in the Files panel, or move files by dragging them between folders. You can also drag a file from the Files panel to the document window to open it, and you can rename, delete, or copy files from within the Files panel.
Properties panel	Displays the properties of the selected element. You can click the expander arrow in the lower-right corner of the Properties panel to display more options. The Properties panel is also commonly referred to as the Property inspector.

Visual aids

Visual aids are page icons, symbols, or borders that are visible only in Dreamweaver. You can turn individual visual aids on and off to make it easier to work with your page elements. To set your visual aids, choose a visual aid from the Visual Aid list on the Document toolbar, as shown in Exhibit 1-4. To toggle all visual aids on or off, press Ctrl+Shift+I.

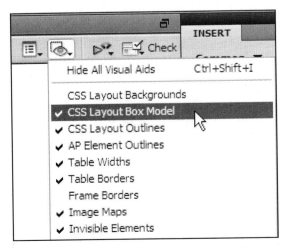

Exhibit 1-4: The Visual Aids list on the Document toolbar

Tabbed documents

You can have multiple documents open simultaneously and switch between them by clicking the document tabs. You can also display documents as floating documents so that each one appears in its own window. To open each tabbed document in a floating window, choose Windows, Cascade. To return a floating window to the standard tabbed format, click the Maximize button in the upper-right corner of any floating window.

Zoom tools

The Zoom tools, which are at the bottom of the document window, enable you to zoom in and out of your pages. For example, using the Zoom tool, click anywhere on the page to "zoom in," or magnify that area. To zoom out, press and hold the Alt key and click on the page. You can also drag a marquee around a specific area of a page to zoom in on that area, or you can select a magnification value from the Zoom list.

Do it!

B-1: Identifying interface components

Here's how	Here's why
1 Click **Start** and choose **All Programs**, **Adobe Dreamweaver CS4**	To start Dreamweaver CS4. If the Default Editor dialog box appears, click OK.
2 At the bottom of the welcome screen, check **Don't show again**	To prevent the welcome screen from appearing the next time Dreamweaver CS4 starts. A dialog box appears, indicating that you can use the Preferences dialog box to enable the welcome screen again.
Click **OK**	
3 Choose **File**, **Open...**	
Browse to the current unit folder	
Open the Outlander Spices folder	
Double-click **index.html**	To open the Outlander Spices home page. Home pages are often named index.html, because most Web servers are configured to look for that file name as the Web site's *root*, or top-level file.
4 Click [Design]	(On the Document toolbar.) To switch to Design view. Split view is the default view.
5 On the menu bar, click **File**	To open the File menu. The drop-down menus in the menu bar contain commands for performing a wide variety of tasks.
With the menu open, point to **Edit**	(The next item in the menu bar.) To view the commands in the Edit menu.
Point to **View**	To view the commands and options in the View menu.
Briefly explore the other menus	
6 Observe the top of the document window	The full path to the open file is displayed for quick reference and verification.
7 Locate the Insert panel	Using the Insert panel, you can quickly add elements to a page. The buttons in the Insert panel are shortcuts to the commands in the Insert menu.
8 Locate the Document toolbar	The Document toolbar contains three buttons that control the current view of the open Web page; click them to switch between Code, Split, and Design views. The toolbar also displays the page title and provides buttons and pop-up menus for frequently used commands.

9	Locate the Properties panel	The Properties panel displays attributes and options for the selected page element.
10	Locate the Files panel	The Files panel displays a list of your files and folders.
11	Click	(On the Document toolbar.) To expand the Visual Aid list.
	From the list, select **Table Borders**	To hide all table borders used in the layout.
12	Show the table borders again	From the Visual Aid list, select Table Borders.
13	Click	The Zoom tool is in the lower-right corner of the document window.

Click as shown

To zoom in on the spices at the top of the page.

14	Click the Zoom list	(In the lower-right corner of the document window.) To display the Zoom list.
	Select **100%**	
15	Click	(The Select tool is in the lower-right corner of the document window.) To return to the default tool.

Workspace layouts

Explanation

Dreamweaver CS4 provides eight preset workspace layouts designed to suit different types of developers or projects. The layouts are Designer (the default), Designer Compact, App Developer, App Developer Plus, Classic, Coder, Coder Plus, and Dual Screen. To switch workspace layouts, select a layout from the workspace switcher, in the top-right corner of the application window, as shown in Exhibit 1-5.

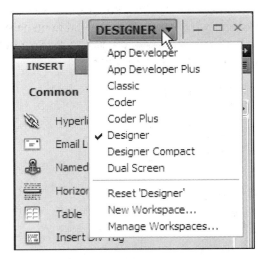

Exhibit 1-5: The workspace switcher menu

Creating a custom workspace layout

In addition to using the default workspace layouts, you can also arrange the workspace to your specific needs and save that layout for later use. To create a custom workspace:

1. Arrange the panels and toolbars in the workspace as desired.
2. From the workspace switcher menu, choose New Workspace. The New Workspace dialog box opens.
3. Enter a descriptive name for the workspace and click OK. The new workspace name appears at the top of the application window.

Exhibit 1-6: The New Workspace dialog box

You can rename or delete custom workspaces by choosing Manage Workspaces from the workspace switcher menu. This opens the Manage Workspaces dialog box, which contains a list of custom workspaces (if any).

Panel groups in the Designer workspace layout

Each workspace layout has a different set and arrangement of panels. The Designer workspace layout displays two panel groups by default: Files and CSS Styles. You can open additional panels in any workspace layout.

The Files panel group

The Files panel group, shown in Exhibit 1-7, contains the Files panel and the Assets panel. The Files panel allows you to quickly open and manage site files and folders. The Assets panel provides easy access to your site assets, such as images, templates, PDFs, and media files. To use the Assets panel, you must first define a local site.

The CSS Styles panel group

The CSS Styles panel group contains the CSS Styles panel and the AP Elements panel. The CSS Styles panel is context-sensitive, allowing you to manage the CSS styles of the selected element. With the AP Elements panel, you can manage properties of absolutely positioned elements (most commonly, `<div>` tags).

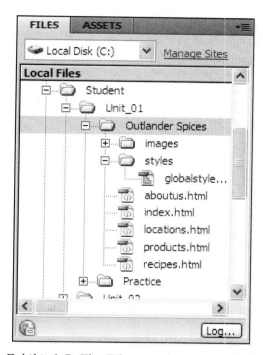

Exhibit 1-7: The Files panel group, with the Files panel active

You can customize the Dreamweaver workspace by showing or hiding panels. To hide or display a panel group, choose Window and then the panel group's name. To expand or collapse a panel group, click its title bar, as shown in Exhibit 1-8. To float a panel group, drag it by its title bar to the desired location.

To resize a floating panel, point to an edge of it. When the pointer changes to a double-sided arrow, drag to resize the panel. You can return a modified workspace to its original layout by choosing Reset *'Workspace Name'* (for instance, Reset 'Designer') from the workspace switcher menu.

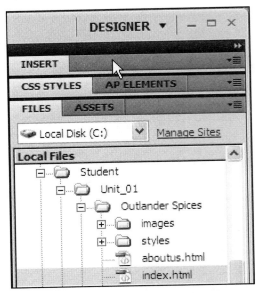

Exhibit 1-8: The Insert panel (collapsed)

Do it!

B-2: Creating a custom workspace

Here's how	Here's why
1 Locate the Files panel	This panel provides quick access to your files and folders.
Click as shown	 (Be sure to click the blank area and not the Assets tab.) To collapse the panel.
Click the blank area at the top of the Files panel again	To expand the Files panel.
2 Drag the Files panel to the left side of the application window	To make the Files panel a floating panel.
3 Point to the right edge of the document window, as shown	 The pointer changes to a double-sided arrow, indicating that you can resize the window.
Drag to the right	To enlarge the document window and narrow the Insert panel.
4 Expand the CSS Styles panel group	Click the panel group's title bar—the area to the right of the AP Elements tab.

5 From the workspace switcher menu, choose **New Workspace...**

To open the New Workspace dialog box.

Type **My workspace**

Click **OK**

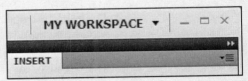

The workspace name appears on the workspace switcher menu. You can return to a saved layout as needed.

6 From the workspace switcher menu, choose **Designer Compact**

In this workspace layout, the panels are reduced to buttons along the right side of the application window.

7 Click as shown

To display the Insert panel as a flyout panel.

Click the **Files** button

To display the Files panel.

8 From the workspace switcher menu, choose **My workspace**

To switch back to your custom workspace.

9 Switch to the default Designer layout

From the workspace switcher menu, choose Designer.

The Properties panel

Explanation

The Properties panel displays the options and properties of the element that's selected in the document window. For example, if you select an image on the page, the Properties panel will display the image's properties, such as its height and width. You can use the Properties panel to observe properties and to set or change properties.

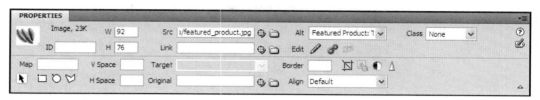

Exhibit 1-9: The Properties panel, with an image selected

When you select page elements other than images and embedded objects such as videos, the Properties panel displays two buttons: HTML and CSS. Click the HTML button to display HTML-related attributes and options, and click the CSS button to display CSS style–related properties and related options.

Do it!

B-3: Working with the Properties panel

Here's how	Here's why
1 On the page, click **In the News**	You'll use the Properties panel to view the attributes for this text.
Observe the Properties panel	The font, style, color, and other attributes of this text are displayed.
2 Click **HTML**	(On the left side of the Properties panel.) To display the HTML attributes of the selected element.
Read the options in the Properties panel	You can apply a class or id attribute, make the text a link, and apply other HTML attributes.
3 In the document window, click the image shown	 To select it.
Observe the Properties panel	It displays the attributes of the selected image.
4 Click as shown	 To hide the Properties panel and display more of the document window.
Show the Properties panel again	Click the area to the right of the Properties tab.
5 On the page, click **Awards**	
In the Properties panel, click **CSS**	(If necessary.) To view the CSS style options for the selected element.

6 Click the Color box, as shown

To open a color palette. The pointer changes to an eyedropper, which you use to select a color.

Click the dark green color shown

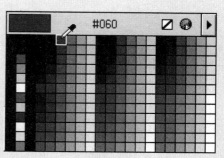

To match the color of the other headings on the page. The text color is now dark green.

Topic C: Basic editing

This topic covers the following Adobe ACE exam objectives for Dreamweaver CS4.

#	Objective
1.6	Describe techniques for making pages accessible.
7.2	Given a media type, insert and deploy that media type into a page.

Editing content

Explanation

Editing content in Design view is a lot like using a word processor. You can click on the page to place the insertion point, and type to insert text. You can also edit, delete, and rearrange text, and insert images, audio files, and video files.

Typical page elements

Web pages can include many types of content, including text, tables, images, and links, as illustrated in Exhibit 1-10.

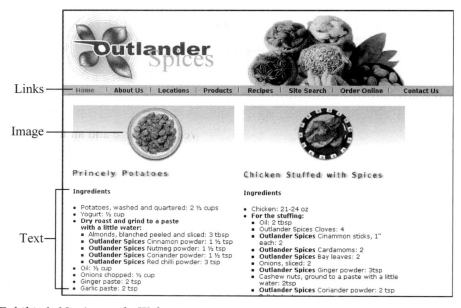

Exhibit 1-10: A sample Web page

The following table describes some typical Web page elements.

Element	Description
Text	Words, phrases, sentences, headings, and paragraphs.
Table	A grid structure consisting of rows and columns, meant primarily to contain tabular data, such as a product list with corresponding prices. Tables can also help you control the layout and spacing of elements on a page.
Image	A graphic file, typically in .gif, .jpg, or .png format. Images can also be used as links.
Link	Text or an image that directs the browser to another location when clicked. The destination might be another Web page, another area of the current page, or some other resource.
Image map	A single graphic that can include multiple links.
Forms	Interactive pages consisting of text input fields, check boxes, and buttons that allow the user to submit data to a server for processing and data storage.

Do it!

C-1: Discussing Web page elements

Questions and answers

1 What are links?

2 What's the difference between an image and an image map?

3 What's a table used for?

4 Have you ever used a form on the Internet? If so, for what purpose?

Text basics

Explanation

To add text to a page, you can simply type at the insertion point, or you can copy and paste text from another source. Inserting and editing text can sometimes cause other elements on the page to move. For example, an image below a paragraph will move down as you add more text to the paragraph.

Do it!

C-2: Inserting and editing text

Here's how	Here's why
1 In the top paragraph, click to the left of **spices**, as shown	heritage of spices from all d specialty stores all over
	To place the insertion point at this location.
2 Type **the finest**	To add text to the paragraph.
Press (SPACEBAR)	To add a space. This type of text editing is similar to working in a word processor.
3 Place the insertion point as shown	**Featured Products**
	Only one product is currently featured, so you'll delete the "s" in "Products."
Press (← BACKSPACE)	To delete the letter.
4 Choose **File**, **Save**	To update the document.

Adding images

Explanation

You can use images to convey or reinforce ideas in ways that text alone cannot. A Web page that includes images is often more visually appealing and inviting to the user than is a page with just text.

To insert an image in a Web page:

1 If necessary, create a subfolder in the site folder and place all the image files in it. Give the folder a logical name, such as "images."
2 In the Files panel, navigate to the folder containing the images for the current site.
3 Drag an image file to the document window.
4 In the Image Tag Accessibility Attributes dialog box, type alternate text and click OK.

You can then adjust the size and position of an image by using the options in the Properties panel.

Alternate text

When you add an image, Dreamweaver prompts you to provide alternate text for the image. Users who have images disabled in their browsers or who use non-visual browsers will be able to read the alternate text and understand its context in the document. If you point to an image that has alternate text, some browsers show the text as a tooltip. Alternate text should describe either the content or the purpose of the image—whichever is most appropriate.

C-3: Adding an image

Here's how	Here's why
1 Scroll to the bottom of the page	You'll insert an image to the left of the Awards heading.
2 In the Files panel, open the images folder	In the Outlander folder, in the current unit folder.
Scroll down in the list of images to locate iso.gif	
Drag **iso.gif** to the left of the Awards heading, as shown	
	To insert the image on the page. The Image Tag Accessibility Attributes dialog box opens.
In the Alternate text box, type **ISO 9000 Award**	Providing alternate text ensures that users with non-visual browsers can access the content.
Click **OK**	To close the Image Tag Accessibility Attributes dialog box.
3 Save the page	

Previewing a Web page

Explanation

As you work on a page, you'll probably want to periodically see it as it will appear in a browser. To preview a Web page in a browser:

1   On the Document toolbar, click the "Preview/Debug in browser" button.
2   From the drop-down list, select a browser.
3   If you have not yet saved your changes, a dialog box opens, prompting you to save your changes. Click Yes to save your changes and preview the page in the selected browser.

Adding browsers to the Preview list

Not all browsers display a Web page the same way—there are often minor differences in how each browser interprets HTML and CSS code, and these differences can affect the way a page looks and functions. For this reason, it's a good idea to preview your Web pages in several popular browsers. When you first install Dreamweaver, it detects the browsers installed on your computer. It uses your default browser as the primary browser for previewing pages. You can add other browsers as needed.

To add other browsers to the Preview list:

1   Choose Edit, Preferences (or press Ctrl+U) to open the Preferences dialog box.
2   In the Category list, select Preview in Browser.
3   Click the plus sign next to Browsers to open the Add Browser dialog box.
4   In the Name box, type a name for the browser.
5   Click the Browse button, and navigate to the .exe file for the desired browser (typically located in a folder in the C:\Program Files folder).
6   Check Secondary browser.
7   Click OK to close the Add Browser dialog box.
8   Repeat steps 3–7 for each browser you want to add to the preview menu.
9   Click OK to close the Preferences dialog box.

Do it!

C-4:   Previewing a page in a browser

Here's how	Here's why
1 On the Document toolbar, click ![Preview/Debug in browser button]	(The "Preview/Debug in browser" button.) A drop-down list appears.
Select **Preview in IExplore**	To view the page in Internet Explorer. A dialog box opens, prompting you to save the changes to the style sheet.
Click **Yes**	(If necessary.) To update the style sheet.
2 Observe your changes and close the browser	

Topic D: Code tools

This topic covers the following Adobe ACE exam objectives for Dreamweaver CS4.

#	Objective
5.1	Configure preferences for Code view.
5.2	Manage code by using Code view.
5.3	Explain how to get information about tags.
5.5	Explain how to select blocks of code in Code view.

Basic HTML

Explanation

As you learned earlier, HTML code defines the basic structure of a Web page. Even if you prefer to work in Design view, you should be familiar with basic HTML syntax.

HTML tags tell a browser how to interpret or display the content enclosed in the tag. For example, the `<h1>` tag identifies a line of text as a level-one heading, and the browser renders it accordingly.

HTML tags are enclosed in angle brackets: < >. Most HTML tags consist of a beginning tag and an ending tag. The ending tag includes a forward slash (/), which tells the browser that the tag instruction has ended. For example, the following code is a snippet of text that uses the `<b>` tag to define bold text:

```
Outlander Spices offers only the <b>best</b> spices.
```

A Web browser would display this text as follows:

Outlander Spices offers only the **best** spices.

The following code shows the basic structure of an HTML document. Notice that some tags are nested inside other tags, and there's an ending tag for each starting tag.

```
<html>
  <head>
    <title>Document Title</title>
  </head>
  <body>
    All rendered HTML and content are inserted here.
  </body>
</html>
```

The standard tags that begin every HTML document are `<html>`, `<head>`, and `<body>`. The `<html>` element is considered the *root element,* or top-level element. All other HTML tags reside within the `<html>` tag. It defines the document as an HTML document. Every HTML document is then divided into two sections: the `<head>` section and the `<body>` section.

The `<head>` section contains the `<title>` element, which defines the document's title. This section also contains style sheet information, meta information, scripts, and other code or resources that aren't rendered on the page.

The <body> section contains all the content (text, images, etc.) that's rendered on a page, along with the code for it. Each tag in the <body> section performs a specific function to define the content. The following table describes a few of the most commonly used HTML tags.

Tag	Description
<a>	Creates a hyperlink to another page or site.
<div>	Defines a section (division) of a page and allows all elements within that section to share formatting attributes.
<span>	Allows you to attach style attributes to an inline section of text, such as specific words or phrases within a paragraph.
<table>	Creates a table.

Document views

As shown in Exhibit 1-11, there are three document view buttons at the top of the document window: Code, Split, and Design. You're already familiar with Design view. You can click the Code button to switch to Code view, for working directly with the HTML code. Click the Split button to split the document window into Code view and Design view.

The Related Files toolbar

Above the document view buttons is the Related Files toolbar, which lists all of the files to which the current page is linked. The example in Exhibit 1-11 shows only one related file, the external style sheet globalstyles.css. (The Source Code button refers to the current document.) You can click any file name on the Related Files toolbar to open that file for editing.

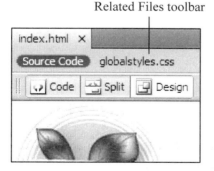

Exhibit 1-11: The view buttons and the Related Files toolbar

Working with code

Dreamweaver provides several tools for selecting and modifying code. In Code view, you can use the Coding toolbar and the Tag Editor to perform common tasks and edit code. In Design view, you can use the Quick Tag Editor to insert and edit code.

The Coding toolbar

When you view a page in Code view, the Coding toolbar appears on the left side of the document window, as shown in Exhibit 1-12. You can use the Coding toolbar to perform common coding tasks, such as indenting code, expanding and collapsing code sections, and adding and removing comments.

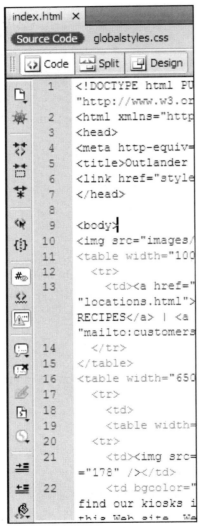

Exhibit 1-12: The Coding toolbar (on the leftmost edge of the Code view window)

The Tag Editor

When you're working in Code view, you can right-click a tag and choose Edit Tag to open the Tag Editor for that tag. In the Tag Editor, you can modify tag attributes, which are sorted by category, and get more information about the tag.

Selecting tags with the tag selector

In both Code view and Design view, you can use the tag selector to select a specific element and its contents. Depending on the current selection or location of the insertion point, the tag selector shows the parent tags, all the way back to the <body> element, as shown in Exhibit 1-13. The tag selector is located in the status bar at the bottom of the document window.

Exhibit 1-13: The tag selector, showing nested tags

The Quick Tag Editor

When you're working in Design view, you can add HTML tags by using the Quick Tag Editor. To insert an HTML tag, click on the page where you want to insert the tag, and then press Ctrl+T. The Quick Tag Editor opens, with a prompt that reads "Insert HTML:", followed by a scrollable list of HTML tags, as shown in Exhibit 1-14. Double-click an element in the list to insert it. You can then add attributes within the Quick Tag Editor, or you can press Enter. If you press Enter, the Quick Tag Editor closes and you can type at the insertion point to insert text inside the new HTML tag.

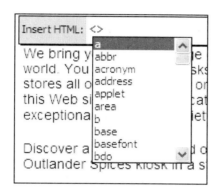

Exhibit 1-14: The Quick Tag Editor

You can also use the Quick Tag Editor to wrap a tag around a selection. Select the text, and then press Ctrl+T to open the Quick Tag Editor. The "Wrap tag:" prompt appears. Double-click an element in the list, and then press Enter.

Selecting text in Design view

There are several ways you can select text for editing or formatting:

- Drag across the text you want to select.
- Click a word twice to select the whole word.
- Click three times anywhere in a paragraph to select that paragraph.

Do it!

D-1: Working with the code tools

Here's how	Here's why
1 Click [⌃ Split]	(On the Document toolbar.) To split the document window into Code view and Design view.
2 In Design view, click an image on the page	To select it. Code view automatically highlights the code that defines the selected object.
3 Click [<> Code]	To switch to Code view.
4 Locate the `<head>` tag What's the purpose of this element?	
5 Locate the `<body>` tag What's the purpose of this element?	
| 6 Under the `<body>` tag, right-click the first **table** tag | ```
<body>
<img src="images/logo
<table width="100%" h
    Edit Tag <table>...
    Insert Tag...
href  Functions
```<br><br>A shortcut menu appears. You can use this menu to access a variety of commands and options. |
| Choose **Edit Tag <table>** | To open the Tag Editor for the `<table>` tag. You can right-click any tag in Code view to open the Tag Editor, where you can modify attributes and get more information about the tag. |
| Observe the options | You can modify a tag's attributes, which are grouped in separate categories. |
```

7 Click as shown

(At the bottom of the dialog box.) To open a reference window.

Briefly scroll through the reference window

You can get information about the selected tag and view usage examples.

Click **Cancel**

To close the dialog box without making any changes. The entire `<table>` tag, with all of its content, is selected, even if you cancel out of the Tag Editor.

8 Click anywhere in Code view

To deselect the `<table>` element.

9 Triple-click the **<table>** tag

To select the entire line of code—only the line, and not the entire block defined by the `<table>` tag.

Press SHIFT

Click to the right of the closing `</table>` tag, as shown

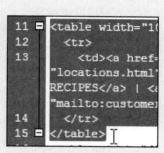

(At line 15.) To select the `<table>` element and the content it contains.

Release SHIFT

10 On the Coding toolbar, click

(The Collapse Full Tag button.) To collapse everything between the opening and closing `<table>` tags. You might find it helpful to collapse certain code blocks if you want to focus on other areas of code.

Click as shown

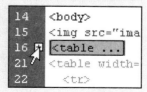

To expand the selection.

11 Click Design

To switch to Design view. Notice that the table that contains the navigation bar is selected.

12 Under "In the News," click anywhere in the first paragraph	To place the insertion point.

In the tag selector, click **<p>**, as shown	
	`<body> <table> <tr> <td> <table> <tr> <td> <p>`
	`PROPERTIES`
	
	To select the paragraph element and its content. The paragraph is selected on the page. Use the tag selector when you want to select an element and its content.

Switch to Code view	Notice that the paragraph tags are selected in addition to the content they contain. Typing over this selection will replace the paragraph tags as well as the content.
Switch to Design view	
13 Triple-click the paragraph shown	this Web site. We are dedicated to providing spices exceptional quality and variety. Discover a whole new world of flavor, look for an Outlander Spices kiosk in a store near you!
	To select the whole paragraph.
Switch to Code view	Notice that only the text content is selected and not the paragraph tags that contain it.
Switch to Design view	
14 Press (CTRL) + (T)	To open the Quick Tag Editor. You can use this tool to insert HTML tags in Design view.
15 In the list of tags, double-click **b**, and then press (↵ ENTER)	To wrap the selected text inside a <b> tag, which makes the text bold.
Click anywhere on the page	To deselect the paragraph.
16 Save and close the page	

Unit summary: Getting started

Topic A   In this topic, you learned about the Internet, the Web, and HTML. You learned that HTML and XHTML are standard **markup languages** used to build Web pages, and that Dreamweaver uses XHTML code by default.

Topic B   In this topic, you identified the main components of the **Dreamweaver CS4 workspace**, including the Properties panel and several other panels. You learned how to switch between **workspace layouts** and create a custom workspace layout.

Topic C   In this topic, you learned how to perform basic **text editing**, and you learned how to **insert an image**. You also learned how to **preview** a page in a browser.

Topic D   In this topic, you learned how to use the **code tools**, and you learned more about HTML tags, including basic HTML syntax. You also learned how to **select text** on a page and select code in Code view. Finally, you learned how to use the **Tag Editor** to modify HTML elements, and you used the **Quick Tag Editor** to insert HTML tags in Design view.

Independent practice activity

In this activity, you'll insert text and an image and preview the page in Internet Explorer. Then you'll use the Quick Tag Editor to wrap an HTML tag around a selection.

1 From the current unit folder, open the Practice folder.

2 Open index.html and save it as **Myindex.html**.

3 In the area to the left of the first paragraph, insert the peppers.jpg image. (It's in the images folder.)

4 In the text at the top of the page, drag to select the sentence beginning with "Discover."

5 Press Ctrl+T to open the Quick Tag Editor, and wrap the selection in a paragraph tag. (*Hint*: Scroll down in the list, double-click "p," and press Enter.)

6 Switch to Code view to verify that the first block of text is not contained in a paragraph tag. Then switch back to Design view.

7 Use the Quick Tag Editor to wrap the first block of text in a paragraph tag.

8 Save the page and preview it in Internet Explorer.

9 Close the browser to return to Dreamweaver.

10 Close all open files.

Review questions

1 How can you hide table borders?

     A Right-click inside the table and choose Table, Hide Table Borders.

     B Double-click the table border.

     C Select the table and choose View, Hide Table Borders.

     D Deselect the Table Borders option in the Visual Aids list on the Document toolbar.

2 How can you add an image to a page?

   A Drag the image file from the Files panel to the document window.

   B In the Files panel, right-click the image and choose Insert.

   C Choose File, Import; navigate to the location of the image file; and click OK.

   D In the Files panel, double-click the image file.

3 How can you view the code for a document? [Choose all that apply.]

   A Press Ctrl+`

   B Click the Code button at the top of the document window.

   C Press F5.

   D Click the Split button at the top of the document window.

4 You're viewing a page in Design view. How can you view the Coding toolbar?

   A Switch to Code view.

   B Choose View, Toolbars, Coding.

   C Choose Window, Code Inspector.

   D Choose View, Code View Options, Coding.

5 In Code view, how can you collapse a selected tag? [Choose all that apply.]

   A Choose Modify, Collapse Full Tag.

   B On the Coding toolbar, click the Collapse Full Tag button.

   C Double-click the tag.

   D To the left of the tag, click the small minus sign (-) .

6 True or false? To add HTML tags to a page, you need to work in Code view.

7 How can you select an entire paragraph, but not its containing HTML tag? [Choose all that apply.]

   A Use the tag selector.

   B Drag to select the paragraph.

   C Triple-click anywhere inside the paragraph.

   D Double-click anywhere inside the paragraph.

8 What's the keyboard shortcut for opening the Quick Tag Editor?

   A Ctrl+Q

   B Shift+T

   C Ctrl+T

   D Ctrl+E

Unit 2

Web sites and pages

Unit time: 60 minutes

Complete this unit, and you'll know how to:

A Plan and define a Web site, and work with the Files panel and the Assets panel.

B Create a Web page, import text from external files, set page properties, and insert special characters.

C Use the Find and Replace dialog box to update content and code.

Topic A: Creating a Web site

This topic covers the following Adobe ACE exam objectives for Dreamweaver CS4.

#	Objective
2.1	Given a scenario, create a site.
2.2	Locate files associated with a Dreamweaver site.
2.3	Manage files associated with a Dreamweaver site.
3.4	Configure local, testing, and remote servers.
7.1	Manage assets by using the Assets panel.

Site planning and organization

Explanation

Organizing site files in a logical structure is critical to the successful operation of your Web site. A good site structure makes it easier to maintain the site efficiently over time.

Planning

Before you begin creating a Web site, it's generally wise to plan it carefully first. Think about how best to structure your pages and content, how you want to present information, and how you want the site to look (color schemes, fonts, and so on) before you begin working on individual pages. Spend some time defining the audience for the site and the goals you want to accomplish.

Effective design also results in easier maintenance. Content requirements, design changes, and job assignments typically change over time. You should plan and design a site that will be easy for another developer or team of developers to take over.

Site structure

A well-designed site must have an effective navigation scheme. You need to plan the link relationships between the pages in your site. Sometimes you can prevent problems by drafting a site flowchart, similar to the simple example in Exhibit 2-1.

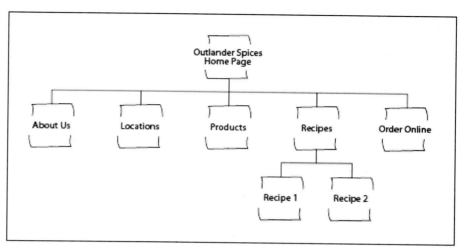

Exhibit 2-1: A flowchart for the Outlander Spices site

You should also keep all the files you plan to use in the site in a logical, organized folder structure. Exhibit 2-2 shows a typical folder structure for a Web site. All images are stored in their own folder, as are style sheet files. You might also have separate folders to store resources such as PDF files, videos, and scripts.

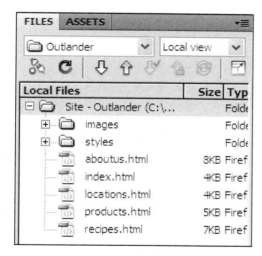

Exhibit 2-2: The Files panel, showing a typical folder structure for a site

Local, remote, and testing sites

When planning a site, you should define three folders for your site files, as described in the following table.

Folder	Location	Purpose
Local	Your local hard disk	To store work in progress. You transfer files from the local site to the other sites when they're complete.
Remote	The Web server where your site is published	To make your site available to your intended audience.
Testing	Any computer, including your PC, the Web server, or a testing server	To test your connection to databases and to test dynamic pages (pages that change according to information received from databases or page variables).

The local folder on your computer is where you work on the site before you publish it on the Internet. After you verify that it looks and functions as you intend, you can publish it to a remote folder on the Web server that hosts your site. If your site includes *dynamic content* (pages or information that can change in response to information received from databases, user activity, or other variables), then you should also define a testing folder.

A local site serves as the root directory for your Web site. When you define the site's root folder, don't use the root of your hard drive or the Dreamweaver application folder.

To define a local site:

1 Choose Site, New Site to open the Site Definition dialog box, shown in Exhibit 2-3.
2 In the Site name box, enter a name for the site.
3 In the Local root folder box, enter the URL for the site. You can click the folder icon to the right of the box to navigate to the folder.
4 Click Next and complete the screens for the Site Definition dialog box. The last screen displays a summary.
5 Click Done to create the site.

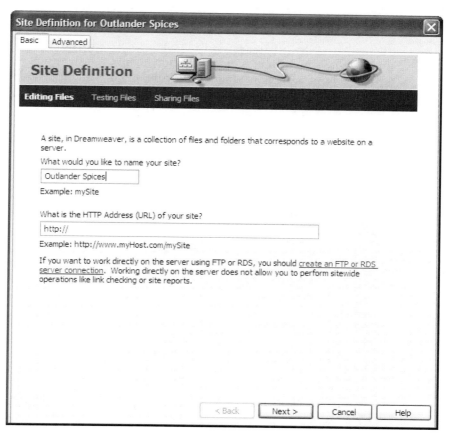

Exhibit 2-3: The Site Definition dialog box

The Assets panel

You can keep track of your site's assets (such as images, styles, scripts, and videos) by using the Assets panel. The Assets panel, shown in Exhibit 2-4, displays a list of images in your site (by default) and information about each file, such as its dimensions, file size, file type, and path. You can click the buttons on the left side of the panel to view other types of assets in the site.

You can drag and drop files from the Assets panel to insert them in a page, just as you can from the Files panel. This provides an alternate way of locating, organizing, and working with your site files. However, you cannot delete files from within the Assets panel. By default, assets are listed alphabetically, but you can also sort them by size, file type, or other categories by clicking a category's column heading.

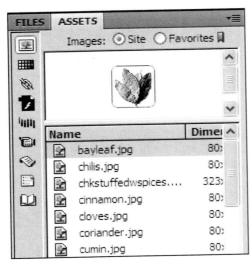

Exhibit 2-4: The Assets panel

Do it!   ## A-1:   Defining a local site

Here's how	Here's why
1 Choose **Site**, **New Site…**	To open the Site Definition dialog box.
Activate the Basic tab	If necessary.
2 For the site name, enter **Outlander Spices**	To name the site. As you type, the name appears in the title bar of the dialog box.
Click **Next**	
3 Verify that **No**, **I do not want to use a server technology** is selected	
Click **Next**	
4 Verify that **Edit local copies on my machine** is selected	
Click 🗀	To open the "Choose local root folder for site Outlander Spices" dialog box.
5 Browse to the Outlander Spices folder	In the current unit folder.
Open the folder and click **Select**	To specify where the files for this site should be stored.
6 Activate the Advanced tab	You'll observe the settings for remote and testing servers.
In the Category list, select **Remote Info**	
Display the **Access** list	To observe the options for connecting to a remote server.
Select **None**	You don't need to connect to a remote server for this activity.
7 Activate the Basic tab	To continue setting up the local site.
Click **Next**	The Summary screen appears.
8 Click **Done**	To create the site.

9 Observe the Files panel

Outlander Spices is listed as a Web site.

Click as shown

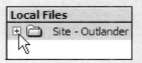

To expand the Site folder.

Observe the contents of the Site folder

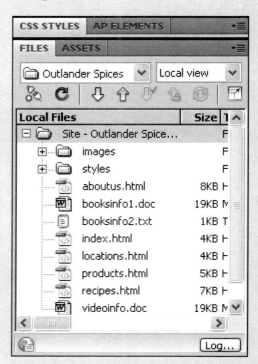

The Site folder contains several files, as well as an images folder, for storing the site's image files, and a styles folder, for storing style sheets.

10 Click **videoinfo.doc**

To select it.

Click it again

So that you can rename the file.

Type **videos.doc**

To rename the file.

11 Select the Assets panel

(At the top of the Files panel group, click Assets.) By default, the site's images are displayed in the Assets panel.

Click ▦

To display the colors used in the site.

Click ▨

To display a list of the site's images again.

12 Use the horizontal scrollbar to view the image details

(At the bottom of the Assets panel.) You can also detach the panel and enlarge it to see more of the information provided in the Assets panel.

13 Click any image in the Assets panel	To select it. A preview of the image appears at the top of the panel.
Select another image	To preview it. The Assets panel provides an alternative to the Files panel for locating specific resources and getting information about them.
14 Click **Name**	(The column heading just above the first image in the list.) To sort the images in reverse alphabetical order.
Click **Name** again	To sort the images in alphabetical order again.
15 Select **bayleaf.jpg**	
Press ⌷DELETE⌷	Nothing happens because you can't delete files from within the Assets panel. To delete or move files, you need to use the Files panel.
16 Right-click **bayleaf.jpg** and choose **Locate in Site**	To locate this asset in the site. The Files panel is activated, and the bayleaf.jpg image is selected in the images folder. In larger sites with a lot of assets, this command can help you find files quickly.
17 Collapse the images folder	Click the minus sign next to the folder.

Topic B: Creating pages

Explanation

Dreamweaver provides several options for creating new Web pages. You can create pages from scratch, or you can use layout templates.

Blank pages and templates

Depending on the nature of your site and your own development preferences, you might choose to start from scratch, or you might prefer to have some of the work done for you before you get started.

To create a new Web page, choose File, New. This opens the New Document dialog box, which displays several options, described in the following table.

Option	Description
Blank Page	You can create a new, blank HTML page that contains only the basic document structure with no content. You can also create a blank page that contains dummy content in a preset layout that you can modify to suit your needs. In the Blank Page category of the New Document dialog box, you can also create CSS documents, XML documents, and many other document types.
Blank Template	This set of options provides HTML templates, plus templates for server technologies such as ASP.NET and ColdFusion. These templates are attached to predefined CSS style sheets, which provide a layout framework that you can build on.
Page from Template	This option shows a list of your own templates from which you can create pages.
Page from Sample	This option provides several basic style sheets that you can use and modify.

Starting with a blank HTML page

To create a blank HTML page:

1   Choose File, New to open the New Document dialog box.
2   Select Blank Page (if necessary).
3   In the Page Type list, verify that HTML is selected (at the top of the list).
4   Click Create.

Page titles

You should give every page a title. Titles appear in the title bar of the browser window and are used by many search engines to provide accurate search results. Exhibit 2-5 shows the title of a page viewed in several browsers. To specify a page title, enter it in the Title box on the Document toolbar.

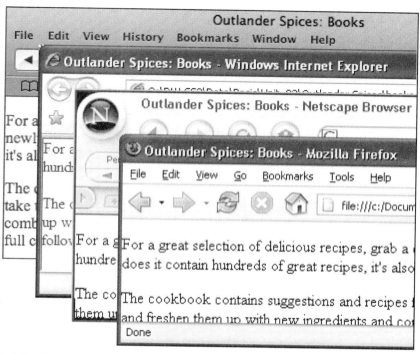

Exhibit 2-5: Page titles as they appear in four different browsers

Do it!

B-1:   Creating and titling Web pages

Here's how	Here's why
1 Choose **File**, **New…**	To start creating a Web page. The New Document dialog box appears.
Verify that **Blank Page** is selected	
Verify that **HTML** and **\<none\>** are selected	In the Page Type list and the Layout list, respectively.
Click **Create**	To open a blank HTML page.
2 On the Document toolbar, edit the Title box to read **Outlander Spices: Books**	Title: Outlander Spices: Books To give this new page a title. This text will appear in the browser window's title bar.
3 Choose **File**, **Save**	The Save As dialog box appears because this is a new document that hasn't been saved yet.
Edit the File name box to read **books.html**	File name: books.html
Click **Save**	
4 Verify that books.html appears in the Files panel list	

Inserting and importing text

You can add text to a Web page by typing in the document window. If the text is in a separate file, you can import the text or copy and paste it into Dreamweaver.

It's often helpful to use an external file as the source of your Web site text, so you can distribute the file for editing and approval by other members of a development team. When the text is approved and ready, you can copy and paste it into a Web page. You can use Dreamweaver to import text from a text file or from a formatted document, such as a Microsoft Word file.

Importing text

When you import text from an external document into Dreamweaver, the Insert Document dialog box appears, prompting you to specify your import and formatting preferences.

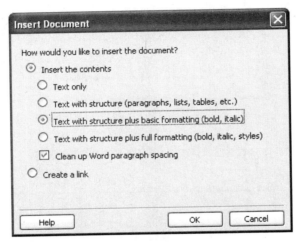

Exhibit 2-6: The Insert Document dialog box

The options in the Insert Document dialog box are described in the following table.

Option	Description
Insert the contents	Copies the file's text into the Web page.
Text only	Inserts plain text without any formatting.
Text with structure	Inserts plain text and retains structures such as paragraph breaks, lists, and tables.
Text with structure plus basic formatting	Inserts plain or structured text. If any text uses basic formatting, such as bold or italics, Dreamweaver retains this formatting by adding basic HTML tags when necessary.
Text with structure plus full formatting	Inserts plain or structured text and retains all HTML tags and internal CSS styles.
Clean up Word paragraph spacing	Removes extra spacing above and below paragraphs in documents imported from Microsoft Word.
Create a link	Inserts a hyperlink to the text file (rather than inserting the text itself).

Pasting text from other sources

Using the standard Copy and Paste commands is another way to bring content from another application into Dreamweaver. To control how Dreamweaver formats content pasted from another application, choose Edit, Paste Special. The formatting options in the Paste Special dialog box, shown in Exhibit 2-7, are the same as those in the Insert Document dialog box, shown in Exhibit 2-6.

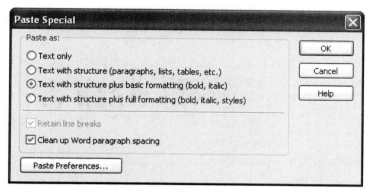

Exhibit 2-7: The Paste Special dialog box

B-2: Importing text

Here's how	Here's why
1 Drag **booksinfo1.doc** from the Files panel to the document window	The Insert Document dialog box appears. You'll import text from this Microsoft Word file and then from a simple text file.
2 Verify that **Insert the contents** is selected	You'll insert the contents of the Word document into the page.
Verify that **Text with structure plus basic formatting (bold, italic)** is selected	To import the text and any basic formatting.
Verify that **Clean up Word paragraph spacing** is selected	To remove unnecessary spaces, carriage returns, and other unwanted characters from the Word document.
Click **OK**	To insert the text as specified. Notice that "Outlander Cooking!" appears in italics—the basic formatting was retained.
3 Switch to Code view	
Observe the text	Dreamweaver uses <em> tags to create the italic text that was in the Word document.
Switch back to Design view	
4 Place the insertion point as shown	ew ingredients and combinat easy-to-follow instructions.|
	If necessary.
Press (↵ ENTER)	To start a new paragraph.
5 Drag **booksinfo2.txt** below the current text	(From the Files panel.) To add more text from another type of file. The Insert Document dialog box appears.
6 Click **OK**	To insert the text and close the Insert Document dialog box. This is a plain text file with no formatting.
7 Save the page	

Page properties

Explanation

With the Page Properties dialog box, you can customize basic design aspects of a page, such as the font, font size, and background color. To open the Page Properties dialog box, click the Page Properties button in the Properties panel, or choose Modify, Page Properties.

When you use the Page Properties dialog box to apply styles, they will be applied to only the current page. When you want multiple pages to share the same styles, you need to use a style sheet.

Page margins

A *page margin* is the space between the content on a page and the edges of the browser window. (Margins may also exist between individual elements.) Browsers apply their own default page margins, typically between 10 and 15 pixels of space on all four sides of the browser window. It's important that you set your own page margins to ensure that your page margins are consistent in different browsers.

You can also set your page margins to zero so that some of your content, such as a navigation bar or header logo, can appear flush with the edge of the browser window. You can then apply margins to large content sections or individual elements to ensure that other content is offset from the browser window's edge and other page elements.

Background color

By default, Web pages have a white background, but you can apply any background color. To do so, select a color from the Background color box in the Page Properties dialog box. Clicking the Background color box opens a *color picker*—a palette with a set of color swatches, as shown in Exhibit 2-8. By default, the color picker displays the Web Safe Colors, a standard set of 216 colors supported consistently by various operating systems.

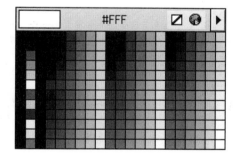

Exhibit 2-8: The color picker

Hexadecimal values

When you point to a color swatch, a three- or six-digit hexadecimal code for the color appears at the top of the color picker, as shown in Exhibit 2-8. Computer monitors use combinations of red, green, and blue to create the colors you see, and the hexadecimal scheme specifies combinations of those colors: the first two characters represent the intensity of red, the next two of green, and the last two of blue.

Hexadecimal notation uses the scale 0123456789ABCDEF, with 0 representing almost no color and F representing 15 times the intensity of 0. Hexadecimal values always start with the pound sign (#). The code #000000 (the lowest level of red, green, and blue) represents black, while #FFFFFF (the fullest intensity of red, green, and blue) represents white. To create yellow, you would add red and green, but no blue, so the hex code would be #FFFF00.

Hexadecimal codes that consist of only three values, such as #FFF or #3BA, are a shortcut for value pairs. The full values would be #FFFFFF and #33BBAA, respectively. Color values that do not consist of three matching pairs, such as #4BC9AE, cannot be reduced in this way.

Setting a default text color

Text is black by default. You can change the color of text that you select on a page, or you can set a default color for all text on a page by using the Page Properties dialog box. You might want to do this if your Web site uses a colored background that makes black text difficult to read or if you just want to establish a complementary color scheme.

Whenever you apply text colors and background colors, you should always make sure that there's sufficient contrast between them to allow for easy reading. Insufficient contrast can strain the eyes and make reading difficult.

Do it!

B-3:   Setting page properties

Here's how	Here's why
1 In the Properties panel, click **Page Properties...**	To open the Page Properties dialog box. You'll use it to set basic style attributes for the current page.
In the Category list, verify that **Appearance (CSS)** is selected	You will apply styles by using CSS, instead of HTML attributes.
2 Click the Background color box	A color picker appears. The pointer changes to an eyedropper.
Click as shown	(In the bottom-right corner.) To apply a pale yellow color.
3 Click the Text color box	To open the color picker.
Select a dark green color	
Click **Apply**	To apply the changes without closing the dialog box. The page now has a pale yellow background, and the text is dark green.
4 In the Left margin box, enter **20**	To give the page a left margin of 20 pixels.
5 In the three other margin boxes, enter **20**	To set the margin to 20 pixels on all four sides of the page.
6 Click **OK**	To apply the changes and close the Page Properties dialog box.
7 Save and close the page	

Special characters

Explanation

Some characters that you might need in your content are not included on a computer keyboard, such as the copyright symbol (©) or language-specific characters like the umlaut (ü). You can insert these special characters in Code view by entering their corresponding *character entities*, which are HTML codes that begin with an ampersand (&) and end with a semicolon. The following table lists some common examples.

Character	Symbol	HTML code
Copyright	©	`&copy;`
Registered trademark	®	`&reg;`
Degree	°	`&deg;`

Inserting special characters

The codes required for these special characters aren't always intuitive or easy to remember, so Dreamweaver provides a list of hints. To insert a special character:

1 In Code view, place the insertion point where you want the special character to appear.
2 Type & (ampersand). A list of hints for special characters appears.
3 Scroll through the list to find the desired character. The HTML code for the character appears in the right column in black, and the character appears in the left column in blue.
4 Select a character from the list.

Extra spaces

When you're working in Design view, you can't insert more than one standard space between words. To insert more than one space, you need to switch to Code view and use the *non-breaking space* character (` `). This special character adds a single space without forcing a line break.

Do it!

B-4:   Inserting special characters and spaces

Here's how	Here's why
1 Open index.html	(From the Files panel.) You'll create a copyright symbol in the page footer.
2 Switch to Code view	
Scroll to the bottom of the page	You'll replace the word "Copyright" with the copyright symbol.
Double-click **Copyright**	ter">`Copyright` Outlander To select it. (You can also drag to select it.)
3 Type **&**	A list appears, showing a variety of special characters.
4 Type **co**	The copyright symbol is selected in the list. (You could also scroll through the list to locate the character you're looking for.)
5 Press (↵ ENTER)	To insert the copyright symbol.
6 Switch to Design view	The text is replaced with the copyright symbol.
7 In Code view, place the insertion point before "All," as shown	Spices. `|`All rights You'll insert spaces after the copyright notice.
Press (SPACEBAR) four times	To insert four spaces in the HTML code.
8 Switch to Design view	The ordinary spaces entered in the HTML code don't have any effect.
9 Switch to Code view and delete the four spaces	(Press Backspace four times.) You'll insert non-breaking spaces instead.
10 Type **&**	To display the list of special characters.
Type **nb**	To select nbsp; from the list.
Press (↵ ENTER)	To insert a non-breaking space.
11 Insert three more non-breaking spaces, as shown	t leader in quality spices.</p> 07. ** **|All
12 Switch to Design view	The four non-breaking spaces create additional space between the two copyright statements.
13 Save the page	

Topic C: Using Find and Replace

This topic covers the following Adobe ACE exam objective for Dreamweaver CS4.

#	Objective
5.4	Find and replace code in Code view.

Finding and replacing content and code

If you need to convert multiple instances of a particular word, phrase, or code, you can use the Find and Replace dialog box. Using Find and Replace can help you save time and prevent omissions. You can find and replace content and code within a single document, a selection, a specific folder, or an entire site.

To find and replace content or code:

1 Choose Edit, Find and Replace. (You can also press Ctrl + F.) The Find and Replace dialog box opens.

2 From the Search list, select an option, depending on what you need to find and replace.

3 In the Find box, enter the text or code you want to find.

4 In the Replace box, enter the replacement text or code.

5 Click Find Next. The first instance of the item you're looking for is selected (if it exists).

6 Click Replace to replace the selection with the replacement text or code.

7 Click Find Next to continue, click Replace All to replace all instances of the item, or click Close to close the dialog box.

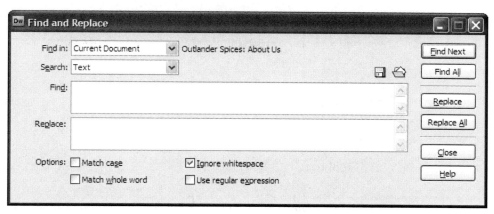

Exhibit 2-9: The Find and Replace dialog box

If you choose Source Code from the Search list, Dreamweaver switches to Code view when you initiate the search. You can also choose the Text (Advanced) option, which allows you to focus your search on tags that are inside (or *not* inside) other HTML tags that you specify. Finally, you can select Specific Tag to search for and replace tags that contain specific attributes or attribute values.

Do it!

C-1: Finding and replacing content and code

Here's how	Here's why
1 Switch to Code view	
2 Choose **Edit**, **Find and Replace...**	To open the Find and Replace dialog box. You'll replace the text "Copyright" with the code for the copyright symbol in every other page in the site.
From the Find in list, select **Entire Current Local Site**	
In the Search list, verify that **Source Code** is selected	
3 In the Find box, type **Copyright**	
In the Replace box, type **©**	
4 Click **Find Next**	The aboutus.html page opens with the text "Copyright" selected.
Move the dialog box so that you can view the selection on the page	If necessary.
Click **Replace**	To replace the text with the character entity for the copyright symbol. The locations.html page opens with the search text selected.
5 Click **Replace All**	A dialog box opens, warning that this command cannot be undone in documents that are not currently open.
Click **Yes**	To replace all instances of the word "Copyright" with the code for the copyright symbol, in every document in the site. The bottom of the dialog box indicates the number of changes made.
6 Observe the Results panel	(At the bottom of the application window.) The Search tab is active, and displays a list of the replacements made in documents that are not currently open.
Right-click the **Search** tab	
Choose **Close Tab Group**	
7 Switch to Design view	
Scroll down to the bottom of the active page	(If necessary.) The copyright statement now begins with the copyright symbol.

8 Choose **File**, **Close All**	To close all open documents. A dialog box prompts you to save before closing.
Click **Yes** until all files are closed	To update each file.

Unit summary: Web sites and pages

Topic A

In this topic, you learned basic **site planning** concepts, and you learned how to define a local Web site. You also learned how to use the **Files panel** to manage your site files and folders, and use the **Assets panel** to view your site's assets, such as images and colors.

Topic B

In this topic, you learned how to create and title Web pages. You learned how to **import text** from other sources, and set **page properties**, including page margins, text color, and background color. Finally, you learned how to insert **special characters** and non-breaking spaces.

Topic C

In this topic, you learned how to use the **Find and Replace** tool to replace content and code. You learned that you can replace code in a document, a selection of text or code, a folder, or an entire Web site.

Independent practice activity

In this activity, you'll define a Web site, create a page, and add text to it. Then you'll set page margins and save the page.

1 Choose **Site**, **New Site** to open the Site Definition dialog box.

2 Enter **Outlander Practice** as the site name, and click **Next**. Click **Next** again.

3 On the Editing Files, Part 3 page, navigate to the Practice folder in the current unit folder.

4 On the Sharing files page, choose **None** as the server connection. Click **Next** and click **Done**.

5 Create a new, blank page and title it **Outlander Spices: Videos**.

6 Save the page as **videos.html**.

7 Import the text of videos.doc into the videos.html page. Use the structure plus basic formatting option.

8 Set the left page margin to **30**, and the top page margin to **15**. (*Hint*: In the Properties panel, click Page Properties.)

9 Give the page a light background color of your choice. (*Hint:* In the Page Properties dialog box, click the Background color box and select a color.)

10 Save and close videos.html.

11 Open index.html and scroll to the bottom of the page. You'll change the text of the copyright footer on every page in the site.

12 Use the Find and Replace dialog box to replace all instances of the copyright symbol with **All Contents ©**, as shown in Exhibit 2-10. (*Hint*: From the Find in box, select Entire Current Local Site, and from the Search box, select Source Code.)

13 Save and close all open files.

All contents © Outlander Spices. All rights reserved.

Exhibit 2-10: The modified copyright statement.

Review questions

1 Which of the following are things to consider when you start to plan a site? [Choose all that apply.]

    A Who your target audience is

    B How you want the site to look

    C How best to structure your pages and content

    D How big you can make the site

2 The Assets panel displays which of the following? [Choose all that apply.]

    A The images in the Web site

    B The folders in the Web site

    C The colors in use in the Web site

    D The HTML files that make up the Web site

    E The script files in the Web site

3 How can you add a title to a page?

    A Double-click the page and enter the title in the Page Title dialog box.

    B Choose Insert, Page Title, and enter the title in the Page Title dialog box.

    C Enter the title in the Page Title box in the Properties panel.

    D Enter the title in the Title box on the Document toolbar.

4 How can you open the Page Properties dialog box? [Choose all that apply.]

    A Double-click the page.

    B In the Properties panel, click the Page Properties button.

    C Ctrl+click the page.

    D Choose Modify, Page Properties.

5 What's the keyboard shortcut to open the Find and Replace dialog box?

    A Ctrl + R

    B Ctrl + F

    C Alt + R

    D Alt + F

Unit 3

Structure and style

Unit time: 60 minutes

Complete this unit, and you'll know how to:

A Define a basic page structure, and create and modify lists.

B Create CSS style sheets, apply styles to text, and create and apply class styles.

Topic A: Structure

This topic covers the following Adobe ACE exam objective for Dreamweaver CS4.

#	Objective
1.3	Explain how to mitigate page weight.

Document structure

Explanation

Headings, paragraphs, and other structural elements allow you to organize a Web page into a logical hierarchy, which can make your pages more searchable, easier to read, and easier for other developers to modify. A well-designed page structure can also make it easier to design and arrange your page content and make your content accessible to users with alternative browsing devices.

Good authoring habits

There are many ways to build a Web page, but it's important that you use HTML tags in their proper context to define a meaningful page structure. For example, if you want to create a heading for a page or a section, you should define the text as a heading and not simply change the appearance of the text to *resemble* a heading. The heading level you choose should logically reflect the nature of the content.

So, for a heading that serves as the top-level heading on a page, you should define it as Heading 1. To do so, select the text, and in the Properties panel, select Heading 1 from the Format list. In the code, the text will be defined by the `<h1>` tag. You can also manually enclose the text in an `<h1>` tag if you prefer to work in Code view.

Creating meaningful and logical document structures establishes consistency on your pages, saves you time and effort when you later update your pages, and allows your pages to be indexed by search engines more efficiently. Focusing on establishing a meaningful document structure typically results in an efficient document with a small file size, or "page weight," especially when all style-related information is contained in an external style sheet. The smaller the file size, the faster the page will load.

Headings and paragraphs

When you're creating a document that requires multiple headings and subheadings, think of it as a traditional outline. HTML includes six headings that you can use to structure your documents. The tags for these headings are <h1> through <h6>. Each has its own default formatting, which you can customize with CSS.

All headings are bold by default, and they use different font sizes. The <h1> tag applies the largest default font size, and the <h6> tag applies the smallest default font size. For example, if you're creating a page intended to deliver company news, an effective structure might look something like this:

```
<h1>Company News</h1>
<p>First paragraph of Company News...</p>
<p>Second paragraph of Company News...</p>
<h2>Subheading of Company News</h2>
<p>First paragraph of subtopic...</p>
```

To define a block of text as a paragraph, click inside the text block and select Paragraph from the Format list in the Properties panel. If you need to divide a block of text into separate paragraphs, simply place the insertion point where you want to begin a new paragraph and press Enter.

Do it!

A-1: Defining headings and paragraphs

Here's how	Here's why
1 Choose **Site**, **New Site...**	You'll define a new Web site.
For the site name, enter **Structure**	
Click **Next**	
Click **Next**	The Editing Files, Part 3 screen appears.
2 Click ⬜	
Browse to the current unit folder	
Open the Outlander Spices folder and click **Select**	
Click **Next**	The Sharing Files screen appears.
3 From the top list, select **None**	
Click **Next**	
4 Click **Done**	To create the site.
5 Open aboutus.html	From the Files panel.
Click the text **About us**	(At the top of the page.) To place the insertion point in this line. This text is defined by a paragraph tag.
6 In the Properties panel, from the Format list, select **Heading 1**	To convert the text to a level-one heading.
7 In Code view, observe the heading code	The text is now enclosed in `<h1>` tags to define it properly as a top-level heading.
Switch to Design view	
8 Convert "About our spices" to a level-two heading	(Click the text and choose Heading 2 from the Format list in the Properties panel.) This heading is not quite as large as Heading 1.
9 Convert the "Spice blends…" line to a level-two heading	
10 Convert "Expansion project" to a level-two heading	

11 Switch to Code view

    Observe the first block of text | The text block is not defined by any HTML tag. You'll define it as a paragraph.

    Switch to Design view

12 Click anywhere inside the first text block | To place the insertion point.

    Observe the Format list in the Properties panel | The Format list reads "None" because this text is not defined by any HTML element.

13 From the Format list, select **Paragraph** | Nothing appears to happen, but the text block is now defined as a paragraph.

    Switch to Code view | Note that the text is now contained in a \<p\> tag. It's important that you always put your text content inside a paragraph tag or another HTML tag, depending on the nature of the content.

    Switch back to Design view

14 Click before the second-to last sentence, as shown

> Outlander Spices ope[
> provide the highest qu
> throughout the USA a
> United States, and we
> few years. |Outlander
> Oregon, and we have

(In that same paragraph.) To place the insertion point.

    Press (↵ ENTER) | To create a new paragraph.

    Switch to Code view | You created a separate paragraph simply by pressing the Enter key.

15 Switch back to Design view

    Define the remaining text blocks as paragraphs

16 Save and close aboutus.html

Lists

Explanation

HTML provides three types of lists: unordered, ordered, and definition. In an unordered list, a bullet, circle, square, or other icon precedes each list item. By default, an unordered list uses bullets, as shown in Exhibit 3-1. Use an unordered list when the sequence of the list items is not important or relevant.

Our most popular spices include:

- Bay leaf
- Cinnamon
- Coriander
- Nutmeg
- Turmeric

Exhibit 3-1: An unordered list

In an ordered list, a number or letter indicates each item's order in the list, as shown in Exhibit 3-2. By default, ordered lists are numbered 1, 2, 3, and so on. You can also choose Alphabet Large (A, B, C), Alphabet Small (a, b, c), Roman Large (I, II, III), or Roman Small (i, ii, iii). Use an ordered list when the sequence of items is important.

Directions:

1. Whisk the yogurt with the paste. Mix well.
2. Heat the oil, reduce the heat, and then add onions, ginger and garlic.
3. Add the potatoes and fry until golden brown.
4. Add the yogurt paste.
5. Cook for 5 minutes.
6. Add ¾ cup of warm water. Bring to a boil and reduce heat.
7. Cook until the potatoes are tender and the gravy is thick.

Exhibit 3-2: An ordered list

You can also create a definition list, which doesn't use bullets or numbers. A definition list is used for terms and their definitions and is often used in glossaries, "frequently asked questions" pages (FAQs), and similar contexts. As shown in Exhibit 3-3, each definition is indented beneath its term. This indentation is the only default formatting that browsers apply to a definition list.

Cinnamon
Cinnamon is one of our most popular spices, due to its sweet flavor and prominent role in baked goods and candies. Cinnamon is also wonderful in stews and sauces.
Nutmeg
Nutmeg comes from the seed of a tropical tree. It has a sweet, rich and aromatic flavor that complements meats, vegetables, tomato sauces, and baked goods.

Exhibit 3-3: A definition list

Nested lists

A *nested list* is a list inside another list. For example, a step in a list of instructions might require its own list of sub-steps. To make a nested list, select the content that you want to turn into a nested list, and click Text Indent in the Properties panel.

Do it!

A-2: Creating lists

Here's how	Here's why
1 Open recipes.html	(Double-click the file in the Files panel.) You'll convert ordinary text to ordered and unordered lists.
2 Select all paragraphs between the "Ingredients" and "Directions" subheadings, as shown	Potatoes, washed and quartered: 2 ½ cups Oil: ½ cup Onions chopped: ½ cup Yogurt: ½ cup **Dry roast and grind to a paste with a little water:** Almonds, blanched peeled and sliced: 3 tbsp Outlander Spices Cinnamon powder: 1 ½ tsp Outlander Spices Nutmeg powder: 1 ½ tsp Outlander Spices Coriander powder: 1 ½ tsp Outlander Spices Red chili powder: 3 tsp Garlic paste: 2 tsp Ginger paste: 2 tsp You'll convert these paragraphs to a single unordered list.
3 In the Properties panel, click ⬛	(The Unordered List button.) To change the selected text to an unordered list.
Click anywhere on the page	**Ingredients** • Potatoes, washed and quartered: 2 ½ cups • Oil: ½ cup • Onions chopped: ½ cup • Yogurt: ½ cup • **Dry roast and grind to a paste with a little water:** • Almonds, blanched peeled and sliced: 3 tbsp • Outlander Spices Cinnamon powder: 1 ½ tsp • Outlander Spices Nutmeg powder: 1 ½ tsp • Outlander Spices Coriander powder: 1 ½ tsp • Outlander Spices Red chili powder: 3 tsp • Garlic paste: 2 tsp • Ginger paste: 2 tsp To deselect the text. The paragraphs are converted to items in an unordered list, which is a more appropriate structure for this content.

4 Switch to Code view

Observe the code for the unordered list

Each item in the list is defined by the `<li>` tag, and all of the list items are nested inside the `<ul>` tag, the unordered list tag.

Switch to Design view

5 Select the paragraphs under "Directions," as shown

> Whisk the yogurt with the roasted paste. M
>
> Heat the oil: reduce the heat, add onions, gi
>
> Add the potatoes and fry until golden brown
> water. Bring to a boil, reduce heat, and coo
> `<body>`

You'll convert these paragraphs into an ordered list.

6 In the Properties panel, click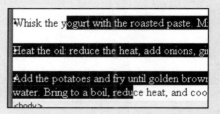

(The Ordered List button.) To convert the text to an ordered list.

Deselect the text

Directions:

1. Whisk the yogurt with the roa
2. Heat the oil: reduce the heat,
3. Add the potatoes and fry unt
   heat, and cook until the potat

(Click anywhere on the page.) To view the results. The text is now an ordered list with three sequential steps.

7 Select all list items from **Almonds** to **Red chili powder**, as shown

- **Dry roast and grind to a paste with a little water:**
- Almonds, blanched peeled and sliced: 3 tbsp
- Outlander Spices Cinnamon powder: 1 ½ tsp
- Outlander Spices Nutmeg powder: 1 ½ tsp
- Outlander Spices Coriander powder: 1 ½ tsp
- Outlander Spices Red chili powder: 3 tsp
- Garlic paste: 2 tsp
- Ginger paste: 2 tsp

You'll indent these list items to create a nested list.

8 In the Properties panel, click

(The Text Indent button.) To indent this part of the list, creating a nested list. The items are indented and have a different default bullet style. You can change the bullet type for a list.

9 Choose **Format**, **List**, **Properties...**

To open the List Properties dialog box.

From the Style list, select **Square**

To change the bullets for the nested list to squares.

Click **OK** and deselect the text

- **Dry roast and grind to with a little water:**
  - Almonds, blanche
  - Outlander Spices
  - Outlander Spices
  - Outlander Spices
  - Outlander Spices
- Garlic paste: 2 tsp
- Ginger paste: 2 tsp

To apply the new bullet style to the selected items.

10 Save and close recipes.html

Topic B: Cascading Style Sheets

This topic covers the following Adobe ACE exam objectives for Dreamweaver CS4.

#	Objective
1.3	Explain how to mitigate page weight.
8.2	Create styles for typography and positioning by using the CSS Styles panel and the Properties panel.
8.4	Create and attach style sheets to pages.
8.5	Explain the behavior of inheritance with respect to styles and style sheets.

Introduction to CSS

Explanation

Cascading Style Sheets (CSS) is the standard style language for the Web. Using CSS rules, you can fully control the design and layout of your pages. For example, you can control the fonts, margins, spacing, colors, and borders that produce your site's look and feel. What makes CSS especially powerful is that you can link multiple pages to a style sheet, and therefore update all of your pages by changing the style rules in one file.

Control and efficiency

Using a CSS style sheet to define a site means that you can focus on content and structure in your documents, without using unnecessary formatting attributes that were typical of old HTML development techniques. Style sheets mean zero redundancy; all of your site's style-related information is stored in a single location instead of being repeated on each page. This leads to faster, simpler design updates and cleaner, more efficient pages that load quickly and consistently.

Internal and external style sheets

You can define and apply styles for HTML elements by using external or internal style sheets, or both.

- **External style sheet** — You define styles in a text file saved with a .css extension. Then, link your Web pages to the style sheet. Use external style sheets whenever you want the style to be global—when you want the styles to apply to multiple pages in a site. When you change a style in an external style sheet, the change is reflected in every page linked to that style sheet.

- **Internal style sheet** — You define styles in the <head> section of an individual Web page. Internal styles apply only to the page in which they're defined. Use an internal style sheet when you need a style for only a single page or when you want to override a style in an external style sheet.

Style types and syntax

The most common types of CSS styles are described in the following table.

Style type	Description

Element styles	These styles define the formatting of HTML elements. An element style overrides the default formatting for that HTML element. The syntax to define an element style is:
	
	`element { property: value; }`
	
	For example, if you want paragraphs to appear in bold type, you'd write:
	
	`p { font-weight: bold; }`

Class styles	Class styles allow you to give elements names that are meaningful to you. For example, you can create a class of the `<p>` element named "important" that applies bold, red text. Any paragraphs that are given that class name will appear with those styles. You can apply class styles to multiple elements on a page. The syntax for a class style is:
	
	`.className { property: value; }`
	
	The class name must begin with a period. For example, to create the rule mentioned above, you'd write:
	
	`.important { font-weight: bold; color: red; }`
	
	A semicolon must separate each style property. A style rule can contain any number of properties.

ID styles	ID styles also allow you to create and name your own elements. However, while a class style can be applied to multiple elements in a page, an ID style can be applied to only one element in a page. ID styles are particularly useful for defining major content sections. For example, you might use a `<div>` element named "navigation" to define a navigation bar, or use a `<div>` element named "footer" to define the page footer. The syntax for an ID style is:
	
	`#IDname { property: value; }`
	
	The ID name must begin with the pound sign (#). For example:
	
	`#footer { font-size: 10px; color: gray; }`

Do it!

B-1: Discussing style sheets

Questions and answers

1 What's a style sheet?

2 What are the two main types of style sheets?

3 What are the advantages of using an external style sheet?

4 When might you want to use an internal style sheet?

5 How can using external style sheets help reduce the size of your HTML files?

6 Name three types of styles you can define in a style sheet.

7 If you want the text of *all* level-one headings in your site to be blue, what type of style should you use?

8 Describe a scenario in which you'd want to create a class style.

9 Describe a scenario in which you'd want to use ID styles.

Creating external style sheets

Explanation   To create a new, blank external style sheet:

1   Choose File, New to open the New Document dialog box.
2   Select Blank Page (if necessary).
3   In the Page Type list, select CSS.
4   Click Create.
5   Save the file and name it with a .css extension. (Save it in a folder dedicated to style sheets, inside your site folder.)

Creating CSS rules manually

When you create a style sheet, it opens in Code view. You can begin entering CSS rules manually, or you can create them by using the CSS Styles panel. To create a rule manually, type it on a new line. For example, to create a rule that gives all level-one headings a font size of 24 pixels, you would write:

```
h1 {font-size: 24px;}
```

The element to the left of the braces is called the *selector*—this is the element that will be styled. The styles (one or more properties and their values) must be inside the braces. In this example, the property is font-size, which is followed by a colon. After this comes the property's value, in this case, 24px.

The semicolon is used to separate one style from the next. If a rule has only one style declaration, you don't need a semicolon, but it's a good idea to place one there anyway, in case you decide to add more properties to the rule.

Using the CSS Styles panel

You can modify CSS styles directly in a style sheet, or you can use the CSS Styles panel to view and edit rules, create and delete rules, and attach the style sheet to your Web site's pages. To open the CSS Styles panel, choose Window, CSS Styles.

Exhibit 3-4: The CSS Styles panel, showing one style rule in globalstyles.css

To link a Web page to an external style sheet:

1 Open the Web page.
2 At the bottom of the CSS Styles panel, click the Attach Style Sheet button. The Attach External Style Sheet dialog box opens.
3 Click Browse to open the Select Style Sheet File dialog box.
4 Navigate to the .css file you want to use.
5 Click OK to select the file and close the Select Style Sheet File dialog box.
6 Click OK to attach the file and close the Attach External Style Sheet dialog box.

Do it!

B-2: Creating and attaching an external style sheet

Here's how	Here's why
1 Choose **File**, **New...**	To open the New Document dialog box. You'll create a new, blank style sheet.
Verify that **Blank Page** is selected	
In the Page Type list, select **CSS**	
Click **Create**	An untitled style sheet file opens in Code view.
2 Click at line 4	
Type **body {**	A list of CSS properties appears.
In the list, double-click **background-color**	A color palette appears.
Select the pale yellow color shown	
	To give the \<body\> element (the visible part of the Web page) a pale yellow background color.

3 Choose **File**, **Save**	To open the Save As dialog box.
Double-click the **styles** folder	To open it. You'll save the style sheet in this folder.
In the File name box, type **globalstyles.css**	File name:	globalstyles.css
Click **Save**	To save the style sheet.
4 Choose **Window**, **CSS Styles**	To open the CSS Styles panel.
Click [All]	(If necessary.) To display the style sheet reference.
To the left of the style sheet, click as shown	**All Rules** ├ globalstyles
	(If necessary.) To expand it. The rule you created for the \<body\> element appears.
5 Open index.html	(From the Files panel.) You'll attach the style sheet to this page.
Observe the CSS Styles panel	The style sheet does not appear because this page is not linked to it.
6 Click [⊜]	(The Attach Style Sheet button is at the bottom of the CSS Styles panel.) The Attach External Style Sheet dialog box appears.
Click **Browse**	To open the Select Style Sheet File dialog box.
Open the styles folder	
7 Select **globalstyles.css**	
Click **OK**	To attach the style sheet to this page and close the Select Style Sheet File dialog box.
Verify that **Link** is selected	To create a link to this style sheet.
Click **OK**	To close the Attach External Style Sheet dialog box. The page now has a pale yellow background because the color is applied to the \<body\> element in the style sheet. You'll edit this style in the CSS Styles panel.

8 Switch to Code view

   Locate the link to the style sheet   (Around line 7.) The code now includes a link to globalstyles.css.

   Switch to Design view

9 In the CSS Styles panel, click **body**   To select the body rule. Its one property is displayed.

   Click **#FFC**   To edit this color value.

   Type **#FFF** and press ⏎ ENTER   To change the background color to white. This is one way you can quickly edit style rules.

10 Open products.html   From the Files panel.

   In the CSS Styles panel, click 🔲   To open the Attach External Style Sheet dialog box, which is already populated with the correct path and file name.

   Click **OK**   To attach the page to the style sheet.

11 Save and close products.html   In the next activity, you'll continue to modify the index.html page and the style sheet.

Typography basics

Explanation

There are many typographical styles that you can apply to text, including the font (typeface), font size, font weight (degree of boldness), and font style (italics and underlining).

Font-size units

There are several units of measurement you can use to control font size. The most commonly used are points and pixels. A point is a unit of print measurement that doesn't translate well to the screen. Pixels are a more appropriate choice for display on a Web page. Using pixels typically produces the most consistent results across various browsers and platforms.

Font sets

A *font set* is a list of similar fonts. When you apply a font set, the user's Web browser tries to display text in the first font specified in the set. If the first font isn't available on the user's computer, the browser looks for the second font in the set. If that font isn't available, the browser tries to apply the third font in the set, and so on. A font set should end with a generic font—serif, sans-serif, or mono-spaced. This practice guarantees that even if a user doesn't have any of the fonts listed in your font set, at least the general font type will be used.

The difference between serif and sans-serif fonts is the style in which the letters are formed. A serif font has *flourishes* (decorations) at the ends of its characters, while sans-serif fonts don't, as illustrated in Exhibit 3-5. Mono-spaced fonts are fonts, such as Courier and Courier New, in which each character takes up the same amount of horizontal space. Mono-spaced fonts resemble typewriter text.

Exhibit 3-5: Serif and sans-serif fonts

Creating and applying element styles

If you choose to write CSS rules directly in Code view, you can define the appearance of an HTML element by using the HTML tag name as the selector in the style rule.

To use the CSS Styles panel to create an element style:

1 Open the Web page or style sheet.

2 In the CSS Styles panel, click the New CSS Rule button.

3 From the Selector Type list, select Tag.

4 From the Selector Name list, select the HTML tag (element) to which you want to apply the style.

5 Under Rule Definition, do one of the following:

- Select the style sheet in which you want to write the new style. (This option will not be displayed if the active document is a style sheet.)

- Select (New Style Sheet File) if you want to write the style in a new style sheet.

- Select (This document only) if you want to write the style in the active document. If you select this option with a Web page active, the style will be embedded in the page's <head> section and will be applied to that page only.

6 Click OK.

7 In the CSS Rule Definition dialog box, set the desired attributes for the style.

8 Click OK.

Creating and editing styles in the Properties panel

The Properties panel provides another way to quickly apply new styles to your pages. Click the CSS button, shown in Exhibit 3-6, to display the CSS options. Either select a rule from the Targeted Rule list, or create a new rule. Click the Edit Rule button to open the CSS Rule Definition dialog box for the selected rule. You can also quickly apply some of the most common styles, including font, font size, color, and text alignment.

Exhibit 3-6: CSS rule controls in the Properties panel

CSS style inheritance

An HTML element can inherit the CSS styles of its parent element (the element that contains it). For example, if you apply font styles to the `<body>` element, every element on the page will inherit those styles because the `<body>` element is the parent element of every rendered element on the page. Similarly, if you have a `<div>` tag that contains three paragraphs (`<p>` tags), and you apply font and color styles to the `<div>` tag, those three paragraphs will inherit the styles.

As you apply styles to your pages, you can use inheritance to your advantage. Inheritance helps eliminate redundancy and complexity, resulting in smaller and more efficient style sheets that are easy to update. Inheritance is also referred to as the cascade, hence the name Cascading Style Sheets (CSS).

There are some exceptions to the general rule of style inheritance. Not every CSS property can be inherited, and some elements, like headings, have their own default font sizes. To change the font size of a heading, you need to apply styles directly to the heading tag by creating an element style.

Do it!

B-3: Defining element styles

Here's how	Here's why
1 In the Properties panel, click CSS	To display the CSS options.
Verify that **body** is selected in the Targeted Rule box	Targeted Rule body You'll apply styles to the `<body>` element, and these styles will be inherited by all other elements in the document.
2 From the Font list, select **Verdana**, **Geneva**, **sans-serif**	All text on the page changes to the new font because every element inherits the styles of the `<body>` element, the topmost parent element.
From the Size list, select **12**	Size: 12 pixels To set the size of the body text to 12 pixels. The text on the page is smaller, except for the headings.
3 Why don't the headings inherit the font size of the body rule?	
4 In the CSS Styles panel, click	(The New CSS Rule button.) The New CSS Rule dialog box opens. You'll create a new style for level-one headings.
Under Selector Type, select **Tag**	You'll define an element style, meaning that it applies to all instances of a specific HTML tag.
In the Tag list, select **h1**	(If necessary.) To apply this rule to the `<h1>` element.
Under Rule Definition, verify that globalstyles.css is selected	
Click **OK**	The CSS Rule Definition dialog box opens.
5 In the Font-size box, type **22**	22 To give all level-one headings a font size of 22 pixels.
6 Click the Color box	To open the color palette.
Select a dark green color	
Click **OK**	To apply the new style. The two level-one headings on the page are now green and slightly smaller than their default size.

7 Scroll down the page to view the Awards heading	This heading did not pick up the style because it's a level-two heading, defined by the `<h2>` element.
8 Create a rule for the `<h2>` element	Click the New CSS Rule button. In the New CSS Rule dialog box, verify that Tag is selected, select h2 from the Tag list, and click OK.
9 In the Font-size list, enter **16**	In the CSS Rule Definition dialog box.
Apply a brown text color	Click the Color box and select a brown color from the palette.
Click **OK**	To apply the new element style.
10 Observe the CSS Styles panel	The h1 and h2 rules appear in the style tree, and the properties of the selected rule are displayed.
11 Click **globalstyles.css**	(At the top of the document window.) To view the changes in the style sheet.
View the new CSS code	The styles are written into the style sheet. You can modify the CSS code directly in the style sheet, or you can use the Properties panel and the CSS Styles panel to create and edit styles.
Choose **File**, **Save**	To save your changes in the style sheet.
12 Click **Source Code**	At the top of the document window.
Switch to Design view	

Class styles

Class styles allow you to share styles among different HTML elements and to name your elements, thus giving added meaning to your document structure. For example, let's say you want to apply a style to just one paragraph among several. You can't achieve this by changing the style definition for the `<p>` tag, because that will affect *all* paragraphs. Instead, you can create a class style and apply it to only the paragraph where it's needed.

Class names

Give your class styles meaningful names to make maintenance easier, both for you and for others who might work on the site in the future. For example, a year from now, it'll be easier to determine how a class style was meant to be used if it's named "discount" instead of "class2."

Creating class styles

As with all CSS styles, you can create class styles in internal or external style sheets. To create a class style:

1　Open the Web page or style sheet.
2　In the CSS Styles panel, click the New CSS Rule button.
3　In the New CSS Rule dialog box, under Selector Type, select Class.
4　In the Name box, type a meaningful name. (Class styles must begin with a period, and Dreamweaver automatically adds the period before the class name.)
5　Under Rule Definition, do one of the following:
  • Select the style sheet in which you want to write the new style. (This option will not be displayed if the active document is a style sheet.)
  • Select (New Style Sheet File) if you want to write the style in a new style sheet.
  • Select (This document only) if you want to write the style in the active document. If you select this option with a Web page active, the style will be embedded in the page's `<head>` section and will be applied to that page only.
6　Click OK.
7　In the CSS Rule Definition dialog box, define the attributes for the style.
8　Click OK.

Applying class styles

After you create a class style, you need to apply it to one or more elements. The class styles you create appear in the Targeted Rule list in the Properties panel. To apply a class style, select an element on the page and then select the class style from the Targeted Rule list.

B-4: Creating and applying class styles

Here's how	Here's why
1 Create a new CSS rule	(In the CSS Styles panel, click the New CSS Rule button.) The New CSS Rule dialog box opens.
From the Selector Type list, select **Class**	
In the Selector Name box, type **copyright**	To specify a meaningful name that reflects how the style will be used. Class names begin with a period, but you don't have to type it here because Dreamweaver adds it automatically in the code.
2 In the Rule Definition list, verify that globalstyles.css is selected	
Click **OK**	To open the CSS Rule Definition dialog box.
3 In the Font-size box, type **11**	The copyright class style will apply a font size of 11 pixels.
From the Font-style list, select **italic**	The copyright class style will also make text italic.
4 Click the Color box	To open the color palette.
Select the white color swatch	(The hexadecimal code that appears should be #FFF.) To make the text white. This means you'll need to change the background color so that there's sufficient contrast to read the white text.
5 Under Category, select **Background**	To view the background style options.
Click the Background-color box	To open the color palette.
Select the dark green color **#060**	This dark green color will provide sufficient contrast to read the white text in the copyright statement.
6 Click **OK**	To create the copyright class style.
7 In the document window, scroll to the bottom of the page	
Click in the copyright text	

8 From the Targeted Rule list, select **copyright**	(In the Properties panel.) To apply the new class style to the text. The copyright statement now has a green background, with smaller white text that's italicized.
Switch to Split view	
Observe the code for the copyright text	`<td class="copyright">&copy;`
	The class style is applied by using the `class` attribute. In this case, the copyright text is contained in a table cell (the `<td>` tag.)
Switch to Design view	
9 Observe the CSS Styles panel	All of the properties in the copyright style are displayed.
10 In the Properties panel, click ≡	To center the text in the table cell.
Observe the CSS Styles panel	The text-align property appears at the bottom of the properties list for the copyright style.
11 Create a class style named **navbar**	Click the New CSS Rule button, verify that Class is selected, type "navbar" in the Selector Name box, and click OK.
12 Under Category, select **Background**	
Click the Background-color box	
Select a light green color, such as #6C3	The green color #6C3 is on the right side of the color palette.
Click **OK**	To create the navbar style.
13 Click anywhere on the navigation links at the top of the page	
In the tag selector, click **<td>**, as shown	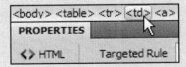
	To select the table cell that contains the navigation links. You'll apply the navbar style to this element.
14 From the Targeted Rule list, select **navbar**	(In the Properties panel.) To apply the new class style to the table cell that contains the links.
15 Save your changes in index.html and globalstyles.css	

16 Choose **File**, **Preview in Browser**, **IExplore**	To preview the page in your browser.
Close the browser, and close all open files in Dreamweaver	

Unit summary: Structure and style

Topic A In this topic, you learned how to apply **structural tags**, including headings and paragraphs. You also learned that an efficient and meaningful page structure can make it easier to maintain a Web site, as well as to design and arrange page content. Then, you learned how to create unordered, ordered, and nested **lists**.

Topic B In this topic, you learned about **Cascading Style Sheets (CSS)**. You learned the differences between internal and external style sheets, and you learned basic CSS syntax. Then you learned how to create an external style sheet and link documents to it. Finally, you learned how to define **element styles** and how to create and apply **class styles**.

Independent practice activity

In this activity, you'll attach a style sheet to several pages, define element styles, and create and apply a class style.

1 Choose **Site, New Site**.

2 Enter **Text Practice** as the site name. Click **Next** twice.

3 On the Editing Files, Part 3 page, navigate to the Practice folder (in the current unit folder).

4 On the Sharing files page, choose **None** as the server connection, and click **Next**.

5 Click **Done**.

6 Open index.html.

7 Attach globalstyles.css to index.html. (*Hint*: The style sheet is in the styles subfolder.)

8 Define the text "Awards" as a level-two heading.

9 In globalstyles.css, create a class style named **mission** that makes text **bold** and **italic**, with a font size of **14 pixels**.

10 Apply the new style to the top paragraph in index.html.

11 Open recipes.html and attach globalstyles.css to it.

12 Define a new CSS style for the `<ul>` (unordered list) element. (*Hint:* In the New CSS Rule dialog box, select **Tag**, and then select **ul** from the Selector Name list.)

13 Set the font size to **12 pixels**, and the text color to a **dark green**. Verify the changes in recipes.html.

14 Define a new CSS style for the `<ol>` (ordered list) element.

15 Set the font size to **12 pixels**, and the text color to a **dark brown**. Verify the changes in recipes.html.

16 Save the page and preview it in your browser. When you're done, close the browser to return to Dreamweaver.

17 Save and close all open files.

Review questions

1 If you want all of the level-two headings in your site to share the same formatting, you should:

   A Create an internal element style for the `<h2>` tag.

   B Create an external element style for the `<h2>` tag.

   C Create an internal class style.

   D Create an external class style.

2 If you want to create a special type of paragraph with extra large text, and you think you'll need to use the style for multiple paragraphs on a page, it's best to:

   A Create an internal element style for the `<p>` tag.

   B Create an external element style for the `<p>` tag.

   C Create an external class style and give it a meaningful name.

   D Create an external ID style and give it a meaningful name.

3 If you want to define a unique section that holds the navigation bar, and you want this element to look the same on every page, it's best to:

   A Create an internal class style and give it a meaningful name, such as navbar.

   B Create an external class style and give it a meaningful name, such as navbar.

   C Create an internal ID style and give it a meaningful name, such as navbar.

   D Create an external ID style and give it a meaningful name, such as navbar.

4 How can you change the font size in a CSS style? [Choose all that apply.]

   A In the CSS Styles panel, select the style. Click the Edit Rule button, make the change, and click OK.

   B In the CSS Styles panel, select the style. Click the value next to font-size in the list of properties, and then edit the value.

   C Double-click some text with the style applied. In the dialog box, change the font size and click OK.

   D Edit the font size directly in the style sheet file.

5 True or false? A class named "introduction" is likely to be more meaningful and effective than a class named "style3."

6 True or false? When you create a style for the `<h1>` element for a page that contains that element, all you need to do is define the style and it's applied automatically.

7 True or false? When you create a class style, the style is automatically applied on the page.

Unit 4

Tables

Unit time: 60 minutes

Complete this unit, and you'll know how to:

A Create tables and nested tables.

B Format rows and cells, merge cells, and add rows and columns to a table.

C Set fixed and variable widths for tables and columns, and change cell borders and padding.

Topic A: Creating tables

This topic covers the following Adobe ACE exam objectives for Dreamweaver CS4.

#	Objective
1.6	Describe techniques for making pages accessible.
4.1	Describe options available for positioning objects.
4.3	Given a visual aid, explain the purpose of and/or when to use that visual aid.

Basic tables

Explanation

An HTML table is a grid structure of rows and columns that you can use to display tabular data, such as products and prices, or to arrange page elements. Tables can be nested inside other tables to create more complex grid structures.

Tables are generally meant for data that's best arranged in rows and columns, such as the information shown in Exhibit 4-1. You can also use tables to arrange page content into a layout, but it's generally best to use CSS to achieve layout and style objectives.

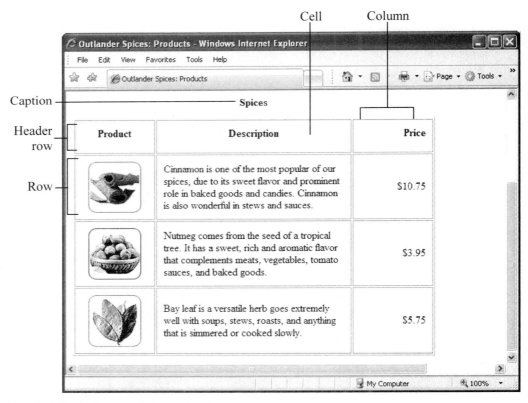

Exhibit 4-1: A simple table used to arrange content

Inserting tables

To insert a table, drag the Table icon from the Insert panel to the page. Then, define the basic table settings in the Table dialog box, shown in Exhibit 4-2. You can then use the Properties panel to change table properties as needed. After you've created a table, you can drag text and images into the cells.

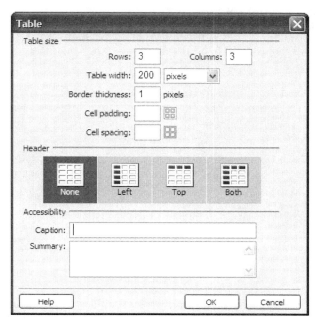

Exhibit 4-2: The Table dialog box

The following table describes the options in the Table dialog box.

Option	Description
Rows	Defines the number of rows in the table.
Columns	Defines the number of columns in the table.
Table width	Defines the width of the table, either in pixels or as a percentage of the browser window or a containing element, such as a `<div>` element.
Border thickness	Defines the width of the cell borders.
Cell padding	Defines the amount of space between a cell's contents and the cell's border.
Cell spacing	Defines the amount of space between adjacent cells.
Header	Defines whether the left column or top row, or both, will be used as row or column headers.
Caption	Defines a title that describes the table.
Summary	Provides a description of the table's contents that can be read by screen readers for the visually impaired.

Visual aids

When you're working with tables, you might find it helpful to enable (or disable) the two table-related visual aids, Table Widths and Table Borders. If you activate the Table Widths visual aid, the current table width is displayed at the bottom of the table, as shown in Exhibit 4-3. You can click the value or the triangles to open a menu of options.

The Table Widths visual aid is active by default. If you want to disable it, click the Visual Aids button on the Document toolbar. A checkmark appears next to each active visual aid. Select Table Widths to disable that visual aid. (If there is no checkmark next to the visual aid, selecting it activates it.)

The Table Borders visual aid draws dotted lines around the table grid so that you can more easily work with the table rows and columns. This visual aid appears only in Design view and will not appear when the page is viewed in a browser.

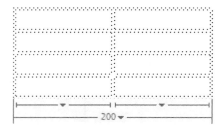

Exhibit 4-3: The Table Borders visual aid and the Table Widths visual aid

Do it!

A-1:   Creating a table

Here's how	Here's why
1 Choose **Site**, **New Site...**	To open the Site Definition dialog box.
2 For the site name, enter **Outlander Tables**	
Click **Next**	
Click **Next**	The Editing Files, Part 3 screen appears.
3 Click 🗀	
4 Browse to the current unit folder	
Open the Outlander Spices folder and click **Select**	
Click **Next**	The Sharing Files screen appears.
5 From the top list, select **None**	
Click **Next**	
Click **Done**	To create the site.
6 Choose **Window**, **Workspace Layout**, **Reset 'Designer'**	To reset the workspace from any changes made to it previously.
Switch to Design view	If necessary.
7 From the Files panel, open products.html	The page is blank. You'll create a basic table and add text and images to it.
From the Insert panel, drag ▦ onto the blank page	The Table dialog box appears.
Edit the Rows box to read **4**	To set the number of table rows to four.
Edit the Columns box to read **2**	To set the number of columns to two.
8 Edit the Table width box to read **580**	To set the table width to 580 pixels.
9 Edit the Border thickness box to read **0**	(Zero.) You'll rely on the Table Borders visual aid to see the table gridlines.

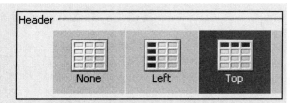

10 Under Header, click **Top**	
	To make the top row of the table a header row.
11 In the Summary box, type **Outlander spices and their descriptions**	To create a brief summary that describes the content of this table for screen readers and other alternative devices.
Click **OK**	To create the table. The table width is shown at the bottom of the table. You'll hide the table width information.
12 On the Document toolbar, click	To expand the Visual Aids list.
Select **Table Widths**	To hide the table width information.
13 Click	To expand the Visual Aids list again.
Select **Table Borders**	To hide the dotted lines that reveal the table gridlines. Without this visual aid, it's difficult to work with the table, so you'll activate it again.
14 Activate the Table Borders visual aid	So that you can see the table gridlines while you work. This border will not appear in a browser.
15 Click in the top-left table cell	To place the insertion point.
Type **Product**	To create a heading for this column. The text in this row is bold and centered in each cell because that's the default formatting of the `<th>` (table header) element, which defines each cell in this row. (You specified the top row of the table as a header in the Table dialog box.)
16 Click in the top-right cell	
Type **Description**	To create a heading for the right column.

17	In the Files panel, expand the images folder	You'll add spice images to the table.
	Drag **cinnamon.jpg** into the cell under "Product," as shown	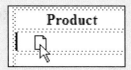
		The Image Tag Accessibility Attributes dialog box appears.
	In the Alternate text box, enter **Cinnamon image**	To specify alternate text for this image. This allows users with non-visual devices, such as screen readers, to understand the content or purpose of the image.
	Click **OK**	To insert the image.
18	Insert **bayleaf.jpg** and **cloves.jpg** into the Product cells, as shown	
		Enter appropriate alternate text for each image.
	Collapse the images folder	(In the Files panel.) To view the files in the Site folder.
19	Open descriptions.txt	(In the Files panel, double-click descriptions.txt.) You'll insert text from this file into the Description column.
	Select and copy the cinnamon description	
	Switch to products.html, and paste the text into the cell next to the cinnamon image	
20	Copy the other descriptions into their corresponding cells in the Description column	Select each description, copy it, and paste it into the appropriate cell. The column width changes as you add the text.
	Close descriptions.txt	
21	Save products.html	

Nested tables

Explanation

A *nested table* is a table that's inserted into the cell of another table. Nested tables give you more flexibility in arranging content, so they're often used to achieve a particular page layout or section layout.

In Exhibit 4-4, for example, the outer table contains all the content shown, and the nested table contains text in cells to be used to create a navigation bar. The outer table consists of one column and two rows. The nested table is placed in the second row of the outer table and consists of one row and six columns.

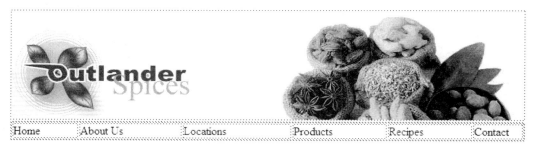

Exhibit 4-4: A nested table used for layout purposes

Do it!

A-2: Creating a nested table

Here's how	Here's why
1 Drag 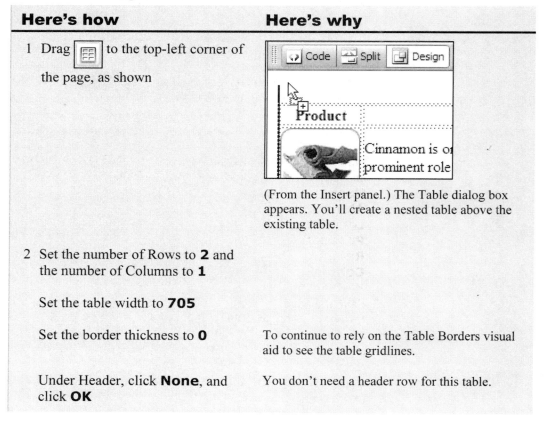 to the top-left corner of the page, as shown	(From the Insert panel.) The Table dialog box appears. You'll create a nested table above the existing table.
2 Set the number of Rows to **2** and the number of Columns to **1** Set the table width to **705**	
Set the border thickness to **0**	To continue to rely on the Table Borders visual aid to see the table gridlines.
Under Header, click **None**, and click **OK**	You don't need a header row for this table.

3 Insert logo.gif in the top row of the new table

In the Alternate text box, type **Outlander Spices logo**

Click **OK**

Collapse the images folder

In the Files panel, expand the images folder, and drag logo.gif into the top row of the table.

4 Drag 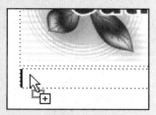 to the bottom row of the table, as shown

To insert another table inside the cell of the existing table. The Table dialog box appears.

Set the number of Rows to **1** and the number of Columns to **6**

Verify that the Table width is set to **705**

Set the border thickness to **0**

5 In the Summary box, type **Layout table for site links**

Click **OK**

To create a summary that describes the purpose of this table.

6 In the six cells of the nested table, enter the following headings:
Home
About Us
Locations
Products
Recipes
Contact

These headings will eventually serve as navigation links.

7 Save the page

Topic B: Table structure and formatting

This topic covers the following Adobe ACE exam objective for Dreamweaver CS4.

#	Objective
4.4	Work with the Properties panel and the Tag Editor.

Basic table formatting

Explanation

Now that you know how to create tables and add text and images to them, you need to learn how to modify a table's structure and apply basic formatting. To do so, you'll need to know how to select table components, and it will be helpful if you're familiar with the table-related HTML tags.

The <table> tag defines a table. Within the <table> tag, each <tr> tag defines a row, and within each row, <td> tags define each cell. The number of cells in a row determines the number of columns in the table. For example, Exhibit 4-5 shows the code for a table consisting of two rows—notice the two sets of <tr> tags—and three columns. The resulting table is shown on the right.

```
<table>
    <tr>
        <td> </td>
        <td> </td>
        <td> </td>
    </tr>

    <tr>
        <td> </td>
        <td> </td>
        <td> </td>
    </tr>
</table>
```

Exhibit 4-5: A simple two-row, three-column table

You can select all the cells in a column or row, or select individual cells. You need to select a row, column, or cell before you can set properties for it.

Selecting individual table cells

The easiest and fastest way to select an individual cell is to press Ctrl and click the cell. You can also click in a cell and then click the rightmost <td> tag in the tag selector at the bottom of the document window.

Selecting rows or columns

To select a row or column, do any of the following:

- Point to the left edge of the leftmost cell (for a row) or the top edge of the topmost cell (for a column). When the pointer changes to a position arrow, click to select the row or column.
- Click the left cell of a row and drag to the right, or click the top cell of a column and drag down.
- (Rows only) Click the cell and then click the rightmost <tr> tag in the tag selector.
- (Rows only) Switch to Code view and select all of the content between a <tr> tag and its corresponding </tr> tag.

Formatting rows

Once you have selected a row, you can use the Properties panel to apply formatting. The row formatting options, shown in Exhibit 4-6, are displayed in the bottom section of the Properties panel. If the bottom section of the Properties panel is not displayed, click the triangle in the lower-right corner of the panel to expand it.

Exhibit 4-6: The row formatting options in the Properties panel

Using row formatting options, you can:

- Merge adjacent cells into a single cell.
- Change the horizontal and vertical alignment of content in the cells in the selected row.
- Change the width and height of the selected row.
- Prevent the text in the cells from wrapping to a new line.
- Define the selected row as a table header row.
- Apply a background color.

Do it!

B-1: Selecting and formatting rows

Here's how	Here's why
1 In the product table, point to the left edge of the top-left cell and click once, as shown	
	(Make sure that the pointer changes to a right-pointing arrow before you click.) To select the row. You'll format this row.
In the H box, enter **30**	(In the Properties panel.) To set the row height to 30 pixels.
From the Vert list, select **Top**	To align the text to the top of the row.
2 Save the page	

Modifying cells

Explanation
There are several ways you can modify table cells by using the Properties panel. When multiple rows or cells are selected, you can merge them. When a single cell is selected, you can split it to create new rows or columns. You can also control cell width, apply background colors to individual cells, rows, or columns, and insert new rows and columns.

Changing cell width

When you change the width of a cell, the entire column is affected. By default, columns are sized according to the largest cell in the column, which is determined by the size of the content it contains. You can also set specific column widths, in pixels or as percentage values.

Specifying background colors

You can specify a background color for rows, columns, and individual cells. To do so, select the row, column, or cell, and then click the Bg box in the Properties panel to open a color palette. Click a swatch to apply its color.

Inserting rows and columns

When a single cell is selected, you can add a row of cells above or below it, and you can add a column to the right or left of it.

To insert a new row in a table, do any of the following:

- Select a cell and choose Insert, Table Objects, Insert Row Above or Insert Row Below.
- Right-click a cell and choose Table, Insert Row. (The row is inserted above the selected cell.)
- Right-click a cell and choose Table, Insert Rows or Columns. In the dialog box, apply the desired settings and click OK.

To insert a column, do any of the following:

- Select a cell and choose Insert, Table Objects, Insert Column to the Left or Insert Column to the Right.
- Right-click a cell and choose Table, Insert Column. (The column is inserted to the left of the selected cell.)
- Right-click a cell and choose Table, Insert Rows or Columns. In the dialog box, apply the desired settings and click OK.

B-2: Adding and formatting columns and rows

Here's how	Here's why
1 In the product table, click the cell containing "Description"	To place the insertion point.
2 Choose **Insert**, **Table Objects**, **Insert Column to the Right**	To add a column to the right of the cell.
3 Set the cell width to **100**	(In the Properties panel, in the W box, enter 100.) Changing the width of the cell affects the entire column. Column widths are set according to the largest cell in the column.
4 In the top cell in the new column, type **Price**	To create a column heading. The text is automatically formatted as a heading, like the other cells in this row.
In the remaining cells, from top to bottom, enter **$10.75**, **$3.95**, and **$5.75**	To enter price data for each spice.
5 Right-click any cell in the top row and choose **Table**, **Insert Row**	To insert a row at the top of the table.
Select the new top row	Point to the left edge of the top-left cell in the Spices table until the pointer turns into an arrow, and then click.
In the Properties panel, click ⊡	To merge the row's cells into a single cell.
6 Click in the merged cell	To place the insertion point in the cell.
Type **Specials**	
In the H box, enter **30**	(In the Properties panel.) To specify a cell height of 30 pixels.
7 In the Properties panel, click the Bg box	To open a background-color palette.
Select the light green color **#66CC00**	To give the cell a light green background.
8 Save the page	

Topic C: Column widths and cell properties

This topic covers the following Adobe ACE exam objective for Dreamweaver CS4.

#	Objective
4.4	Work with the Properties panel and the Tag Editor.

Customizing cells

Explanation

You can control column and table widths in a variety of ways. You can set column widths to a fixed size, or use percentage values to create variable widths. You can also customize cell borders, the space between adjacent cells, and the space between a cell's content and its borders.

Fixed and variable widths

You can set a column's width to a fixed number of pixels or to a percentage of the table width. Similarly, you can set a table's width to either fixed or variable. A variable-width table is sized with a percentage value and is relative to the width of the browser window. You can also combine fixed- and variable-width settings, as described in the following table.

Column width	Table width	Resulting column width
100 pixels	500 pixels	100 pixels
100 pixels	85% (of browser)	100 pixels
10% (of table)	500 pixels	50 pixels (10% of 500 pixels)
10% (of table)	85% (of browser)	8.5% of browser (10% of 85%)

Do it!

C-1: Applying fixed and variable widths

Here's how	Here's why
1 Preview products.html in your browser	You'll change some of the columns from fixed widths to variable widths.
Point to the right edge of the browser window	The pointer changes to a double-sided arrow to enable resizing.
Drag the right edge of the window back and forth	To resize the window. Notice that the tables remain the same size. They have fixed widths, so their size isn't calculated relative to the size of the browser window.
Close the browser	
2 Click in the Product cell	
In the W box, enter **100**	(In the Properties panel.) To set the width of the first column to 100 pixels.
3 In the tag selector, click **\<table\>**	\<body\> \<table\> \<tr\> \<th\> PROPERTIES To select the entire table. You'll change the width of the table from a fixed width to a percentage of the browser window. The options in the Properties panel change with the selection.
In the W box, enter **85**	
From the list next to the W box, select **%**	W 85 % H pixels To make the table width 85% of the width of the browser window.
4 Drag to select from the **Price** header to the last price data cell	Price ue to its $10.75 candies. ith soups, $3.95 d slowly. in the nd Panang. $5.75 back to and are You'll align the price data in this column.

5	From the Horz list, select **Center**	(In the Properties panel.) To align the data in these cells to the right. "Horz" is short for "horizontal alignment."
6	Center the spice images in their cells	Drag to select the cells, and then select Center from the Horz list in the Properties panel.
7	Click in the Description cell	
	From the Horz list, select **Left**	To align this table header to the left of its cell.
8	Save the page and preview it in Internet Explorer	
	Resize the browser window horizontally	Drag the edge of the window back and forth. The product table expands and contracts as the window changes size. However, the right and left columns remain the same size because they still have fixed widths. Depending on the purpose of your tables, you might want to set variable widths.
	Close the browser	
9	Click inside the product table	
	In the tag selector, click **<table>**	To select the product table.
10	Set the table width to 600 pixels	In the Properties panel, enter 600 in the W box, and then select pixels from the adjacent list.

Borders, cell spacing, and cell padding

Explanation

Dreamweaver applies default settings to table borders, the spacing inside cells, and the spacing between cell borders and cell content. You can modify these attributes by selecting the table and then setting options in the Properties panel.

The space between a cell's borders and its content is called *cell padding*. You can change the amount of cell padding by entering a numeric value in the CellPad box in the Properties panel. The space between adjacent cells is called *cell spacing*. You can change the amount of cell spacing by entering a value in the CellSpace box in the Properties panel.

Do it!

C-2: Customizing table cell properties

Here's how	Here's why
1 Select the product table	You'll adjust the cell padding and borders.
2 In the Properties panel, in the CellPad box, enter **10**	To increase the space between each cell's border and its content to 10 pixels.
In the CellSpace box, enter **4**	To increase the space between adjacent cells to 4 pixels. You can see the increased space between the gridlines.
3 Edit the Border box to read **1**	To apply a 1-pixel border.
Edit the CellSpace box to read **0**	To remove the space between adjacent cells.
4 Save the page and preview it in Internet Explorer	
Close the browser	
Close products.html	

Unit summary: Tables

Topic A   In this topic, you learned about **tables**. You learned how to insert a table, create a **header row**, insert text and images, and create **nested tables**.

Topic B   In this topic, you learned how to select and format **cells**, **rows**, and **columns**. You also learned how to **merge cells** and insert rows and columns.

Topic C   In this topic, you learned how to fine-tune **table properties**, including column and table widths, borders, cell padding, and cell spacing.

Independent practice activity

In this activity, you'll create a table from an example.

1 From the Practice folder in the current unit folder, open locations.html.

2 Below the USA image, create the table shown in Exhibit 4-7.

3 Save and close the page.

The shaded states indicate expansion plans over the next five years.

STATE	STORES AND LOCATIONS
Washington	• Seattle Blue Heaven • Sierra Foods, Medford • Shopper's Paradise, Seattle • Tacoma Treasure, Redmond
Oregon	• Port Plaza, Portland • Shopper's Paradise, Portland
Nevada	• All U Need, Reno • Plaza Givo, Las Vegas

Exhibit 4-7: The completed table

Review questions

1 What is a nested table?

   A A table that's inserted into a row of another table

   B A table that's inserted into a cell of another table

   C A table with fixed dimensions

   D A table with flexible dimensions

2 What determines the number of columns in a table?

   A The number of rows

   B The number of column tags

   C The number of cells in each row

   D The value of the column attributes

3 What determines the width of a column?

   A The width you set for the first cell in the column

   B The width you set for the table

   C The width you set for an intersecting row

   D The width of the largest cell in that column

4 A table has a fixed width of 600 pixels. A cell inside this table has a width of 20%, and no other width is specified for another cell in its column. How many pixels wide is this column?

   A 80 pixels

   B 60 pixels

   C 160 pixels

   D 180 pixels

   E 120 pixels

5 What is cell padding?

   A The space between a cell's borders and content

   B The space between cells

   C The space between rows and columns

   D The space between a table and the bottom of the page

6 What is cell spacing?

   A The space between a cell's borders and content

   B The space between adjacent cells

   C The space between rows and columns

   D The space between a table and the bottom of the page

Unit 5

Links

Unit time: 45 minutes

Complete this unit, and you'll know how to:

A Create links to other pages and resources, create named anchors and link to them, and create e-mail links.

B Create an image map.

C Apply CSS styles to link states.

Topic A: Creating links

Explanation

Links provide the functionality that makes the Web the interconnected world that it is. Links enable users to navigate to other pages in a site, to external pages and resources, and to specific sections of a page.

Link types

There are three basic link types:

- *Local* links navigate to other pages and resources in a Web site.
- *External* links navigate to pages and resources outside a Web site.
- *Named-anchor* links navigate to specific sections of a Web page. Named-anchor links are also called *bookmark links* or *intra-document links*.

Local links

Local links are links to pages and resources within a Web site, so specifying the path is relatively simple. If the destination file resides in the same directory as the page that contains the link, you can simply type the file name in the Link box in the Properties panel. If the link destination resides in a different folder, you need to specify the folder name, followed by a forward slash and then the file name.

To create a local link:

1   Select the text or image that you want to serve as the link.
2   In the Properties panel, do one of the following:

- In the Link box, enter the name of the destination file. If the destination file is not in the same folder as the current page, enter the path and file name.
- Next to the Link box, drag the Point-to-File icon to the destination file in the Files panel.
- Click the Browse button and navigate to the destination file.

Do it!

A-1:   Creating a link to a page in your site

Here's how	Here's why
1 Choose **Site, New Site...**	To open the Site Definition dialog box.
2 For the site name, enter **Outlander Links**	
Click **Next**	
Click **Next**	The Editing Files, Part 3 screen appears.
3 Click 🗀	
4 Browse to the current unit folder	
Open the Outlander Spices folder and click **Select**	
Click **Next**	The Sharing Files screen appears.

5	From the top list, select **None**	
	Click **Next**	
	Click **Done**	To create the site.
6	From the Files panel, open aboutus.html	
7	In the top navigation bar, double-click **Home**	To select it. You'll create a link that navigates to the home page.
8	In the Properties panel, in the Link box, enter **index.html**	To make the text "Home" a link to index.html. The file is in the same folder as the current page, so you don't need to specify the path.
	Deselect the Home link	(Click anywhere on the page.) By default, links appear as blue, underlined text to distinguish link text from normal text. You can use CSS to customize link styles.
9	Save aboutus.html	
10	Open index.html	(From the Files panel.) You'll create a link on this page.
11	Triple-click **About Us**	To select the text.
12	Make "About Us" a link to aboutus.html	In the Properties panel, enter aboutus.html in the Link box.
	Save index.html	
13	Preview the page in your browser	(Press F12.) To see the link in action.
	Click **About Us**	The browser navigates to aboutus.html.
14	Click **Home**	The browser navigates to index.html.
	Close the browser	

Named anchors

Explanation

With named anchors, you can mark an element on a page as a target, and then create a link that navigates directly to that target. This technique is often used in pages that are long vertically to make it easier to jump to specific sections. You can also link to a named anchor on another page in your site.

To create a named anchor:

1   From the Visual Aids list, select Invisible Elements (if it's not already active) so that named-anchor tags will be displayed in the document window.

2   Place the insertion point at the target location.

3   In the Insert panel, click the Named Anchor button to open the Named Anchor dialog box.

4   In the Anchor Name box, type a name for the anchor.

5   Click OK.

To link to a named anchor, select the text or image that will serve as the link. Then, in the Properties panel, do one of the following:

- In the Link box, type # (the number sign), followed immediately by the name of the anchor. For example: `#anchorName`.

- Drag the Point-to-File icon to the named anchor.

Do it!

A-2: Creating and linking to a named anchor

Here's how	Here's why
1 Switch to aboutus.html	
2 On the Document toolbar, click [icon]	To open the Visual Aids list.
Verify that Invisible Elements is active	(There should be a checkmark next to it.) This visual aid will display symbols for named anchors.
3 Switch to Code view	You'll add an anchor at the top of the document. Switching to Code view sometimes makes it easier to place the insertion point in a precise location in the document structure.

Click to the right of `<body>`	`</head>`
	
	`<body>`
	
	At the top of the source code.

4 In the Insert panel, click [icon]	(The Named Anchor button.) The Named Anchor dialog box appears.
In the Anchor Name box, type **top**	You'll create a link to this location in the document.
Click **OK**	To insert the anchor.

5   Switch to Design view

    Deselect the anchor

(Click anywhere on the page.) To view the Named Anchor icon. This icon will not appear in a browser—it's displayed only in Design view.

6   Scroll to the bottom of the page and select the text **Go to Top**

You'll make this text a link to the *top* anchor.

    In the Properties panel, in the Link box, enter **#top**

7   Drag the Named Anchor icon next to the "Our Spices" heading

The Named Anchor dialog box opens.

    Type **spices** and click **OK**

To create an anchor next to the heading.

8   Insert a named anchor next to the "Expansion Project" heading

9   At the top of the page, select **Our Spices**

    Create a link to the Spices anchor

10 Make "Expansion Project" a link to the other named anchor

11 Save aboutus.html

12 Preview the page in your browser

    Click **Our Spices**

To go to the Our Spices heading in the page.

    Click the Back button in your browser

    Click **Expansion Project**

To go to the Expansion Project heading.

    Click **Go to Top**

To go back to the top of the page.

13 Close the browser

External links and e-mail links

Explanation

External links navigate to a page or resource on another Web site. You can also create a link that launches the user's default e-mail program, begins an outgoing message, and inserts the e-mail address of your choice in the To field.

To create an external link:

1 Select the text or image that you want to serve as the link.

2 In the Properties panel, in the Link box, type the complete URL of the destination page or resource.

To create an e-mail link:

1 Select the text or image that you want to serve as the link.

2 In the Properties panel, in the Link box, type **mailto:** followed by the recipient's e-mail address.

Do it!

A-3:   Creating external links and e-mail links

Here's how	Here's why
1 Switch to index.html	
2 Select the ISO 9000 award image	
	(Near the bottom of the page.) You'll make this image an external link.
3 In the Link box, enter **http://www.iso.org**	In the Properties panel.
Deselect the image	There's a blue border around the image. By default, browsers draw a blue border around images that are links. You'll disable this border.
4 Select the image again	
In the Border box, enter **0**	(In the Properties panel.) To remove the default border.
Deselect the image	To verify that the blue border is gone.
5 At the top of the page, select **Contact**	You'll make this text an e-mail link.
In the Link box, enter **mailto:info@outlanderspices.com**	
	When the user clicks the link, his or her default e-mail program will open, with this address used for the outgoing message.
6 Save index.html	
Preview the page in your browser	
7 Click **Contact**	An e-mail message with the specified address opens in the default e-mail application. (If no e-mail application is configured on the computer, you're prompted to configure one.)
Close the e-mail message	(If applicable.) Do not save the email.
8 Click the ISO 9000 award image	To view the ISO Web site.
Close the browser	
9 Close index.html	

Topic B: Image maps

This topic covers the following Adobe ACE exam objective for Dreamweaver CS4.

#	Objective
1.6	Describe techniques for making pages accessible.

Creating image maps

Explanation

An *image map* is an image that contains multiple links. Areas within the image, called *hotspots*, are links to other pages, resources, or named anchors. Image maps provide a unique, interactive design tool that you can use in a variety of design contexts.

Defining hotspots

A hotspot in an image map can be any size and any one of several shapes: oval, circle, rectangle, square, or irregularly shaped polygon.

To create an image map:

1 Select the image in the document window.
2 In the Properties panel, in the Map box, enter a unique name for the image map.
3 Click the Rectangular Hotspot Tool, the Oval Hotspot Tool, or the Polygon Hotspot Tool.
4 Drag to draw the outline, or if you're using the Polygon tool, click the corners of the shape to begin the outline.
5 Use the Point-to-File icon or the Browse button to create a local link, a named anchor, or an external link.

Specify alternate text for each hotspot

In an image map, it's important to provide alternate text for the image itself, as well as for each hotspot. Screen readers will be able to read the alternate text for the hotspots in the order in which they appear in the code. Without the alternate text for each hotspot, screen readers will read each entire link address, which can be long and unhelpful to the user of that device.

You can enter alternate text for a hotspot in the Alt box in the Properties panel.

Do it!   **B-1:   Creating an image map**

Here's how	Here's why
1 Open locations.html	From the Files panel. The page contains several named anchors. You'll create links to them in an image map.
Click the image of the U.S.	To select it.
2 In the Properties panel, in the Map box, enter **locations**	To name the map.
3 Click ⬜	(The Rectangular Hotspot Tool is in the Properties panel.) You'll draw a hotspot.
4 Point to **OR**, as shown	(The pointer changes to a crosshair.) You'll insert a hotspot here. When a user clicks the image of Oregon, the browser will go to the specified destination.
Drag over and down to draw a rectangle, as shown	This defines the clickable region for this link. A dialog box appears, reminding you to describe this hotspot for users with alternative devices.
Click **OK**	
5 In the Alt box, type **Oregon**	To provide alternate text for users with screen readers and similar devices.
6 Edit the Link box to read **#Oregon**	Link #Oregon
Press ⏎ ENTER	To create a link from the hotspot to the Oregon anchor.

7 Is the Rectangular Hotspot Tool the most appropriate tool for this hotspot?

Why or why not?

8 Click

(The Polygon Hotspot Tool is in the Properties panel.) You'll create a polygon hotspot.

9 Point to **NV**, as shown

The pointer changes to a crosshair.

Click the top-right corner of the state border, as shown

To set the first point of the hotspot polygon. The dialog box opens, reminding you to provide alternate text for the hotspot.

Click **OK**

10 In the Alt box, type **Nevada**

Click the top-left corner of the state border, as shown

To define the second point of the polygon. A line appears between the two points.

11 Continue clicking each corner until the hotspot takes the shape of the state, as shown

12 Create a link to the named anchor **#Nevada**

Edit the Link box to read #Nevada.

13 Save locations.html

Preview the page in your browser

14 Point to **OR**	A ScreenTip with the alternate text appears.
Click **OR**	To navigate to the Oregon anchor.
Scroll up to display the map	If necessary.
Click **NV**	To navigate to the Nevada anchor. If the Nevada anchor is not displayed at the top of the browser window, the browser window is not large enough vertically. You can see the intended result if you decrease the vertical size of the browser.

15 Close the browser

Topic C: Link styles

Explanation
By default, text links appear as blue, underlined text. These default styles might not work within your site's color scheme. You can apply CSS styles to links to customize their appearance in a variety of ways. You can also assign styles that act as visual cues to the state of a link.

Link states

Link states define the current condition of a link. There are four link states, as described in the following table.

State	Description
Link	The default state of a link that hasn't been activated in any way.
Visited	The state of a link after you click it and its destination page has loaded. In many browsers, visited links appear as purple, underlined text by default.
Hover	The state of a link when you point to it. Most browsers don't apply any default formatting to the hover state.
Active	The state of a link when you click it but haven't yet released the mouse button. A link is in this state for only a moment.

Visited links

The browser's cache keeps track of links whose destinations have been viewed. When a link has been visited, the link remains in that state until the browser's cache is cleared. For example, in Internet Explorer, choose Tools, Internet Options, Clear History to reset the browser's list of visited links.

If you recently viewed the page that a link references, the link appears in the visited state even if you didn't click it.

Creating link styles

You can create link styles manually in a style sheet, or you can let Dreamweaver write the code. To create link styles:

1   In the CSS Styles panel, click the New CSS Rule button.
2   From the Selector Type list, select Compound.
3   From the Selector Name list, select either a:link, a:hover, a:visited, or a:active, depending on the link state for which you're defining a style.
4   In the Rule Definition list, select the style sheet (if necessary), and then click OK.
5   Set the desired styles and click OK.

Do it!   ## C-1: Applying link styles

Here's how	Here's why
1 Observe the links in the navigation bar	The links are blue and underlined. This is the default formatting that most browsers apply to links. Blue text doesn't fit with this site's color scheme, though, and it's hard to read against the green background color.
2 Expand the CSS Styles panel	If necessary.
Click ⊞	To open the New CSS Rule dialog box.
3 From the Selector Type list, select **Compound**	
From the Selector Name list, select **a:link**	
In the Rule Definition list, verify that globalstyles.css is selected	
Click **OK**	To create a style for the default link state. The CSS Rule Definition dialog box appears.
4 From the font-weight list, select **bold**	
Click the Color box and select the dark green color **#060**	
Under text-decoration, check **none**	To remove the default underline.
Click **OK**	To format this link state and close the dialog box. The Home link shows the formatting you specified.
5 Create a CSS rule for **a:visited**	Click the New CSS Rule button in the CSS panel. Then, in the New CSS Rule dialog box, select a:visited from the Selector list, and click OK.
Make the text black	Click the Color box and select the black color swatch in the upper-left corner.
Make the text bold	From the font-weight list, select bold.
Under text-decoration, check **none**	To remove the default underline for the visited state.
Click **OK**	

6 Create a CSS rule for **a:hover**

Make the text bold, remove the underline, and make the text color white

7 Activate globalstyles.css	At the top of the document window, click globalstyles.css.
Press `CTRL` + `S`	To save the style sheet with the changes you made.
8 Preview the page in your browser	Press F12, or choose File, Preview in Browser.
Observe the links	The links that you have visited have the color you applied to the a:visited rule.
9 Point to the links	The link text changes to white.
10 Close the browser	
Save and close all files	

Unit summary: Links

Topic A   In this topic, you learned about **links**. You learned how to create links to pages within a Web site, and you created **named anchors** and linked to them. You also learned how to create **external links** and **e-mail links**.

Topic B   In this topic, you learned how to create an **image map**. You learned how to draw **hotspots** on an image map with various shape tools and link those hotspots to other destinations.

Topic C   In this topic, you learned how to apply CSS styles to **link states**. You learned that applying link styles creates visual cues about the status of links on a page and allows you to fit your links into your color scheme.

Independent practice activity

In this activity, you'll create external links, an e-mail link, and an image map. Then you'll create named anchors and link to them, and apply link styles.

1 Choose **Site**, **New Site** to open the Site Definition dialog box.

2 Enter **Links Practice** as the site name. Click **Next** twice.

3 On the Editing Files, Part 3 page, navigate to the Practice folder in the current unit folder.

4 On the Sharing files page, choose **None** as the server connection, and click **Next**.

5 Click **Done**.

6 Open index.html.

7 For the Home, About Us, Locations, and Contact items in the navigation bar, create links to their corresponding Web pages. For Contact, specify a link to the e-mail address **contact@outlanderspices.com**.

8 Apply link styles of your choice to the links, using the **a:link**, **a:visited**, and **a:hover** selectors.

9 Save your changes and test the links in your browser. Then close the browser and close index.html.

10 Open locations.html.

11 Insert named anchors next to the Washington and California rows in the table.

12 Create polygon hotspots for Washington and California. Specify alternate text for each hotspot, and then link the hotspots to their corresponding anchors.

13 Save locations.html and test the links in your browser.

14 Close the browser and any open files.

Review questions

1 To create a link to a location within a document, you need to:

A Create a local link on a page.

B Create a named anchor and then link to that anchor.

C Create a link from one anchor to another.

D Create a link to a page, and then on that page, create a link back to the original page.

2 The default link state is defined by which selector?

A a:active

B a:link

C a:visited

D a:hover

3 The active state is:

A The default state of a link.

B The state a link enters when you click it.

C The state a link enters when you point to it.

D The state a link enters when it has already been clicked.

4 The hover state is:

A The default state of a link.

B The state a link enters when you click it.

C The state a link enters when you point to it.

D The state a link enters when it has already been clicked.

5 True or false? To make an image map accessible to users with assistive devices like screen readers, you just have to specify alternate text for the image itself.

Unit 6

Image formats and attributes

Unit time: 30 minutes

Complete this unit, and you'll know how to:

A Choose appropriate image formats, insert images, and modify image properties.

B Insert and modify background images, write effective alternate text, and design a page by using a tracing image.

Topic A: Working with images

This topic covers the following Adobe ACE exam objective for Dreamweaver CS4.

#	Objective
1.3	Explain how to mitigate page weight.
1.6	Describe techniques for making pages accessible.

Images on the Web

Explanation

Images are an integral part of Web design. They catch the user's eye, they can introduce a unique artistic aspect to site designs, and they can often deliver information in a way that text can't. For example, images of products give potential buyers visual information that can't be matched by a text description.

File size is a vital consideration when you use images on Web pages. Large image files can take a long time to load in a user's browser. Try to keep your image file sizes as small as possible without sacrificing quality.

File formats

The three main image formats currently supported by browsers are GIF, JPEG, and PNG. GIF images, which can contain a maximum of 256 colors, are best used for images with relatively few colors and with areas of flat color, such as line drawings, logos, and illustrations. GIFs also support animation and transparency. The GIF format isn't recommended for photographs or illustrations with complex color gradations. When you save simple images with fewer than 256 colors, GIF uses a *lossless* compression algorithm, which means that no image data is discarded to compress the image.

The JPEG format supports more than 16 million colors, so it's best for photographs and images that have many subtle color shadings. JPEG uses *lossy* compression, which means that some image data is discarded when the file is saved. You can select the degree of compression applied when saving the file, with the following tradeoff: the smaller the file, the lower the image quality.

The PNG format combines some of the best features of JPEG and GIF. It supports more than 16 million colors, so it's ideal for photos and complex drawings. It can use a variety of lossless compression algorithms, and it supports many levels of transparency, allowing areas of an image to appear transparent or semitransparent.

The following table summarizes these three image file formats.

	GIF	JPEG	PNG
Best used for:	Simple images with few colors	Photographs	Photographs or simple images
Maximum colors	256	More than 16 million	More than 16 million
Compression	Lossless	Lossy	Lossless
Transparency	One level (complete transparency)	Not supported	Multiple levels

Do it!

A-1:   Discussing image formats

Questions	Answers
1 Which image formats are typically best for photographs?	
2 Which image formats support transparency?	
3 True or false: The GIF format and the JPEG format support the same number of colors.	
4 A corporate logo that contains text and six colors is probably best saved in what image format?	
5 Why is it important to limit the file size of your images?	

Image-based text

You can add text to a page in the form of an image. If you have a graphics application, such as Adobe Photoshop, Adobe Illustrator, or Adobe Fireworks, you can create text in a graphics file and save it with the appropriate file extension (typically .gif). Image-based text is often used for logos or headings that require special styling that can't be achieved by using HTML or CSS.

Advantages

By using image-based text, you can take advantage of exotic fonts that visitors aren't likely to have on their machines and would therefore be unable to display. You can also apply special effects, such as drop shadows or embossing, which you can't achieve by using actual text.

Disadvantages

Image-based text has its disadvantages. Using several images on a page increases the page weight and download time. Also, because the images aren't text, the content isn't searchable by search engines or by the browser's Find function. You can minimize this limitation by always providing effective alternate text for your images. For image-based text, your alternate text should duplicate the text in the image.

A-2: Inserting images

Here's how	Here's why
1 Choose **Site**, **New Site...**	To open the Site Definition dialog box.
2 For the site name, enter **Outlander Images**	
Click **Next**	
Click **Next**	The Editing Files, Part 3 screen appears.
3 Click 🗁	
4 Browse to the current unit folder	
Open the Outlander Spices folder and click **Select**	
Click **Next**	The Sharing Files screen appears.
5 From the top list, select **None**	
Click **Next**	
Click **Done**	To create the site.
6 Expand the Site folder	(In the Files panel.) If necessary.

7 Open recipes.html

(From the Files panel.) You'll replace the title of each recipe with an image that uses a script font. When you want to use unusual fonts in your design, you often need to use images.

8 Delete **Princely Potatoes**

Select the text and press Delete.

Expand the images folder

9 Drag **heading-potatoes.gif** to the location of the deleted text

(From the images folder.) The Image Tag Accessibility Attributes dialog box appears.

In the Alternate text box, type **Princely Potatoes**

To give this image alternate text that matches the image's content, so that screen readers can access the content and search engines can index the text.

Click **OK**

To insert the image as the recipe heading.

10 Delete **Outlander Chicken**

Make heading-chicken.gif the new heading

Drag the image above the recipe, on the same line as the Princely Potatoes heading. Type "Outlander Chicken" in the Alternate text box, and click OK.

11 Save recipes.html

Image attributes

When you drag an image onto a page, Dreamweaver writes the HTML code required to embed the image. This code consists of the image tag—`<img>`—and several attributes, which are properties for the element. The location of the `<img>` tag tells the browser where to embed the file, and the `src` attribute tells the browser where to locate the image file. You can set image attributes by using the Properties panel.

The attributes of the `<img>` tag are described in the following table.

Attribute	Use	Description
src	Required	Specifies the path to the image file.
alt	Recommended	Provides alternate text. If the browser can't display the image, alternate text provides access to the text in the image or a description of the image, whichever is more appropriate.
height	Recommended	Specifies the height of the image.
width	Recommended	Specifies the width of the image.
vspace	Optional	Applies additional space on both vertical sides of the image (the top and bottom).
hspace	Optional	Applies additional space on both horizontal sides of the image (the left and right).
align	Optional	Aligns an image with text on the same line.
border	Optional	Specifies the pixel width of the border around an image that acts as a link.

Images and accessibility

You already know how to provide alternate text when you insert images. It's also important to understand the reasons that it's important to do so and to create meaningful and effective alternate text.

Many Internet users need to use alternative browsing software such as screen readers and Braille devices. For example, people who have visual impairments can browse Web content with screen readers, which read aloud the content of a Web page. When a screen reader encounters an image, it obviously can't describe the image. It's up to you, the developer, to describe what the user can't see. Depending on the nature of the image, there are several types of alternate text you can write.

Descriptive and instructive alternate text

Suppose that your page has two images that act as "previous" and "next" links to navigate through an online help system. If these images do not have alternate text, and a user with a screen reader tries to use this help system, the user is likely to get lost or confused. The help system wouldn't be particularly helpful. The user would have no idea that the images are a means of navigation.

Screen readers read aloud any text inside a link, but if an image *is* a link, there's no text to read aloud. In this case, you would want to specify either descriptive or instructive text for the images. For example, "Previous page" would describe the purpose of the image. "Click to view the previous page" would provide instructions.

Descriptive text should describe the content of an image. For example, if you have a picture of an ocean view, your alternate text might be "Picture of an ocean view" or "View from Virginia Beach."

Instructive text should clearly indicate an action that the user should or can take. Other examples of instructive text include "Enter a plain-text version of this Web site" and "Click to disable sound."

Replacement text

Use *replacement text* when your image contains text that you want the user to read. For example, if you have a GIF image that displays the text "BeeHive Record Company," your alternate text should literally replace this content—it should read "BeeHive Record Company."

Additional advantages of alternate text

Alternate text helps all users, not just users with visual impairments. Some browsers display a ScreenTip showing the alternate text when you point to the image. Also, alternate text can help make your pages more searchable and provide more accurate search results.

Use proper punctuation in alternate text

If your alternate text is a complete sentence or is made up of multiple sentences, you should always use proper punctuation. Screen readers use punctuation to emulate the natural pauses and inflections in speech.

A-3: Setting image attributes

Here's how	Here's why
1 Select the image shown	
	You'll specify alternate text for this image.
In the Alt box, enter **Image of Princely Potatoes recipe**	(In the Properties panel.) In this case, it's best to provide a brief description of the image.
2 In the V Space box, enter **10**	To add 10 pixels of space above and below the image.
3 Provide appropriate alternate text for the other recipe image	Select the image, and enter a fitting description in the Alt box in the Properties panel.
4 Give the image 10 pixels of vertical space	
5 Save the page and preview it in your browser	
Close the browser	
6 Close recipes.html	
7 An image of an arrow and the word "download" is intended to prompt users to download a file. What type of alternate text is probably best for this image, and what text would you use?	
8 Suppose you have an image that shows the application window of a new software program. What type of alternate text is probably best for this image, and what text would you use?	

Topic B: Background images

This topic covers the following Adobe ACE exam objective for Dreamweaver CS4.

#	Objective
4.2	Design a page by using a tracing image.

Options for applying background images

Explanation

You can use an image as a background for an element, such as a table, or for an entire Web page.

By default, background images repeat across and downward to occupy an element's entire dimensions. This repetition is called *tiling*. If you're working with a background image for an entire page, the image might tile several times to occupy the space, depending on the size of the image relative to the size of the browser window.

For example, if the image of peppers shown in Exhibit 6-1 is inserted as a background for a table, the image will tile to fill the width and height of the table, as shown in Exhibit 6-2. Choose a background image that doesn't detract from the foreground of the page or make the text difficult to read. For example, the descriptions and prices in Exhibit 6-2 are difficult to read against the underlying peppers.

With CSS, you can prevent an image from tiling so that it appears only once. You can also specify that the image tiles only horizontally or only vertically.

Exhibit 6-1: A background image

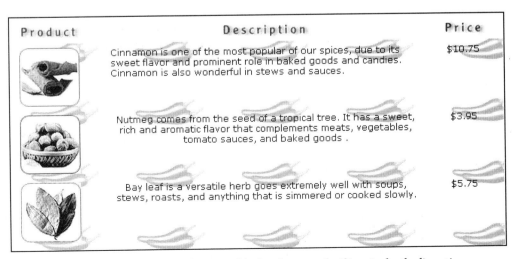

Exhibit 6-2: A small image used as a table background, tiling in both directions

Applying a background image to a page

By using the Page Properties dialog box, you can apply a background image to a page and control how the image tiles on the page. The Repeat list in the Page Properties dialog box contains four options:

Repeat option	Description
no-repeat	Prevents the background image from tiling.
repeat	Tiles the background image both horizontally and vertically. This is the default behavior of background images.
repeat-x	Tiles the background image horizontally.
repeat-y	Tiles the background image vertically.

To apply a background image to the current page:
1. Choose Modify, Page Properties. (You can also press Ctrl+J.)
2. In the Category list, select Appearance (CSS).
3. Click Browse, navigate to the background image file, and click OK.
4. From the Repeat list, select an option. Click OK.

Applying a background image to a page element

You can create a CSS rule that sets a background image, and then apply that rule to a specific element. The CSS Rule Definition dialog box contains additional options for controlling the appearance of a background image, as described in the following table.

Property	Description
Background-position (X)	Sets the horizontal position of the background image: left, center, right, or an integer value that you specify.
Background-position (Y)	Sets the vertical position of the background image: top, center, bottom, or an integer value that you specify.
Background-attachment	Determines whether the background image scrolls with the page content. Options include fixed and scroll (the default setting).

To create and apply a background image by using a class style:
1. In the CSS Styles panel, click the New CSS Rule button.
2. Under Selector Type, select Class.
3. In the Selector Name box, type a class selector name. Click OK.
4. In the CSS Rule Definition dialog box, in the Category list, select Background.
5. Set the desired options and click OK.
6. Select the element to which you want to apply the background image. From the Class list in the Properties panel, select the class name.

If you want to create a page background, create a rule for the <body> element and set the desired background-image styles.

Designing with a tracing image

If you're working with a design mockup that was created in a graphics application, such as Adobe Illustrator or Adobe Photoshop, you can use the mockup as a tracing image. The tracing image appears as a page background in Design view, and you can use it to arrange elements as you build the page. A tracing image is not part of the actual page; it merely serves as a design and layout aid.

To work with a tracing image, open the Page Properties dialog box and select the Tracing Image category, as shown in Exhibit 6-3. Click the Browse button to select a graphic to use as the tracing image, and use the Transparency slider to control the opacity of the image. Reducing the opacity of the tracing image will make it easier to view the content you're working with.

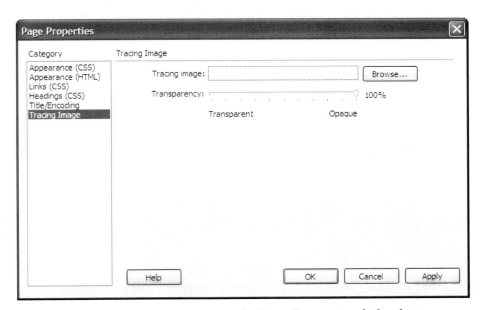

Exhibit 6-3: Tracing image options in the Page Properties dialog box

By default, tracing images are positioned in the upper-left corner of the page. However, you can reposition them by choosing an option from the Tracing Image submenu in the View menu.

Do it!

B-1: Applying a background image

Here's how	Here's why
1 From the Files panel, open index.html	
2 In the CSS Styles panel, double-click **body**	To open the CSS Rule Definition dialog box. You'll edit the CSS rule for the `<body>` element by applying a background image.
3 In the Category list, select **Background**	To view the background style options.
Click **Browse...**	To open the Select Image Source dialog box.
Scroll to the right, select **spicebg.jpg**, and click **OK**	
4 From the Background-repeat list, select **no-repeat**	To prevent the background image from repeating, or "tiling."
5 From the Background-position (X) list, select **right**	To align the background image with the right side of the page.
6 From the Background-position (Y) list, select **bottom**	To align the background image with the bottom of the page.
Click **OK**	
7 Switch to the style sheet and save the changes	At the top of the document window, click globalstyles.css, and then press Ctrl+S.
8 Preview the page in your browser	
Scroll down the page	To view the background image. It has a very low opacity to ensure that it doesn't detract from the readability of the text.
9 At the top of the page, click **About Us**	To navigate to the aboutus.html page.
Scroll down the page	Because the background-image style was applied in the global style sheet, every page shares the background image.
Close the browser	
10 Close all open files	In Dreamweaver.

Unit summary: Image formats and attributes

Topic A   In this topic, you learned about the **GIF**, **JPEG**, and **PNG** image formats. You learned about the advantages and disadvantages of using image-based text, and you learned about the attributes of the image tag. Then you learned how to write effective **alternate text** for your images, based on different situations.

Topic B   In this topic, you learned how to apply **background images**. You learned how to control the positioning and tiling of a background image, and you learned that you can use a **tracing image** to help you design a page around a graphical site mockup.

Independent practice activity

In this activity, you'll replace text with images and apply a background image to a table.

1 Choose **Site**, **New Site** to start the Site Definition dialog box.

2 Enter **Images Practice** as the site name. Click **Next** twice.

3 On the Editing Files, Part 3 page, navigate to the Practice folder in the current unit folder.

4 On the Sharing files page, choose **None** as the server connection, and then click **Next**. Click **Done**.

5 Open aboutus.html.

6 Replace the "Our History" heading with ourHistory.gif. Provide appropriate alternate text for the image.

7 Replace the text "Our Spices" heading with ourSpices.gif. Provide appropriate alternate text.

8 Save your changes in aboutus.html.

9 Create a CSS class rule named **navTable** that applies the background image **greenbar.gif**. Prevent the background image from tiling. (The greenbar.gif image is in the images folder.)

10 Apply the navTable class style to the table containing the navigation links.

11 Save your changes in the style sheet.

12 View the results in your browser. The background image is a green bar that gradually lightens toward its right side.

13 Close all open files.

Review questions

1 Which of the following are advantages of using image-based text? [Choose all that apply.]

   A Image-based text allows you to use exotic fonts and text effects.

   B Image-based text loads faster than normal text.

   C Image-based text can be more eye-catching than normal text.

   D Image-based text is easier to read than normal text.

2 Which of the following are disadvantages of using image-based text? [Choose all that apply.]

   A Too many images increase a page's overall size and download time.

   B The content in the image can't be indexed by search engines.

   C The alternate text you specify for the images can't be indexed by search engines.

   D Text in images is usually harder to read than actual text.

3 When your image contains text, your alternate text should:

   A Describe the content of the image.

   B Duplicate the text that appears in the image.

   C Be omitted.

   D Provide more information about the text.

4 Alternate text for a photograph without text should:

   A Briefly describe the content of the image.

   B Indicate that the image doesn't contain text.

   C Be omitted.

   D Indicate that it's a photographic image.

5 How can you add a tracing image to a page?

   A Press and hold Ctrl, and drag an image to the page.

   B In the Page Properties dialog box, select the Tracing Image category, select the image you want to use, and set options for it.

   C Choose Insert, Image. In the dialog box, select the image you want to use, check Tracing Image, and click OK.

   D Add the image to the page; then right-click the image and choose Convert To Tracing Image.

6 When you insert a background image, how is it tiled, by default?

   A Horizontally

   B Vertically

   C Horizontally and vertically

   D Diagonally

7 In the CSS Rule Definition dialog box, how can you align a non-repeating background image to the top of an element?

A From the background-position (X) list, select top.

B From the background-attachment list, select top.

C From the background-position (Y) list, select top.

D From the background-image list, select top.

Unit 7

Publishing

Unit time: 40 minutes

Complete this unit, and you'll know how to:

A Check file size and download times, check for broken links and orphaned files, cloak files, and validate code.

B Connect to a Web server, and upload and update a site.

Topic A: Site checks

This topic covers the following Adobe ACE exam objectives for Dreamweaver CS4.

#	Objective
1.3	Describe how to mitigate page weight.
2.3	Manage files associated with a Dreamweaver site.
9.3	Identify and fix broken links.

Testing page size and download time

Explanation

Before you upload a site, it's important to verify that your page "weight" isn't excessive. *Page weight* is the total file size of a document and all the resources (images, movies, scripts, style sheets, etc.) that it loads when the page is requested by a visitor. The higher the page weight, the longer it takes to load the page. If your pages load slowly, some users (particularly those with slower connections) might leave your site and seek similar information or services elsewhere.

Dreamweaver calculates the size of an open document by counting up the kilobytes (K) of the document and all the resources that load along with it. You can view the download time of a page at a particular connection speed in the lower-right corner of the document window.

Changing the download time baseline

By default, the connection speed in the status bar is set to 56K, which is a slow baseline by today's standard. You can change this setting in the Status Bar category in the Preferences dialog box.

Do it!

A-1: Checking page size and download time

Here's how	Here's why
1 Choose **Site, New Site...**	To open the Site Definition dialog box.
2 For the site name, enter **Publishing**	
Click **Next**	
Click **Next**	The Editing Files, Part 3 screen appears.
3 Click 🗀	
4 Browse to the current unit folder	
Open the **Outlander Spices** folder and click **Select**	
Click **Next**	The Sharing Files screen appears.

5 From the top list, select **None**

   Click **Next**

   Click **Done**   To create the site.

6 Expand the Site folder   (In the Files panel.) If necessary.

7 Open index.html   From the Files panel.

   In the status bar, observe the page   The page size is around 113K, and the download
   size and download time   time on a 56K modem is about 17 seconds.

8 Open aboutus.html

   In the status bar, observe the page   This page size is approximately 57K, and the
   size and download time   page will take about 4 seconds to load fully over
                                                     a 56K modem. The 56K baseline is low, so
                                                     you'll set it higher.

9 Choose **Edit**, **Preferences...**   To open the Preferences dialog box.

   In the Category list, select   To display status bar options.
   Status Bar

   In the Connection speed list, enter   To set a faster connection speed as the target
   700   baseline. After conducting an audience analysis,
                                                     you have determined that this is closer to the
                                                     average speed with which your visitors access
                                                     your site.

   Click **OK**   To close the dialog box.

10 Check the download time for both   For users connecting at 700K, index.html will
   pages again   download in about 2 seconds, and aboutus.html
                                                     in 1second. If you believe your target audience
                                                     has slower connection speeds, then optimize
                                                     your images or reduce the number of images
                                                     used on your Web site.

11 Close all open pages

Broken links and orphaned files

Explanation

Before you publish a Web site, you should verify that all of the links in the site work correctly. As you build pages, it's often easy to mistype a link or accidentally link to a page that was later deleted or renamed. If users click a broken link, the browser will display an error message indicating that the linked page cannot be found. Having to open each file and test every link would be a time-consuming and tedious development task. Fortunately, Dreamweaver can check the integrity of all of your local and external links for you.

To check links for an entire site:

1 In the Files panel, select a Web site.
2 Right-click in the Files panel and choose Check Links, Entire Local Site. You can also choose Site, Check Links Sitewide or press Ctrl+F8. The Link Checker panel opens.
3 In the Link Checker panel, you can identify and repair broken links, as shown in Exhibit 7-1.
4 From the Show list, select External Links to review all external links.
5 From the Show list, select Orphaned Files to display any orphaned files that might exist in your site.

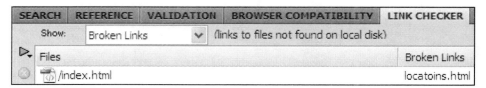

Exhibit 7-1: The Link Checker panel

Orphaned files

You should also check for *orphaned files*, which are files that reside in your site folders but have no pages linking to them. These files might include early drafts of Web pages or image files that you decided not to use. Removing orphaned files from your site before uploading prevents unnecessary bloat on the server and makes site maintenance easier.

Cloaking

Sometimes you might have orphaned files that you don't want to remove from the site. For example, you might have text documents or original image files, such as those in the Photoshop .psd format, that you might want to access later. Keeping them with the site folder makes them easier to locate.

Cloaking folders or file types allows you to store them in your site, but prevents them from being included in normal site operations, such as link reports or uploading functions. To cloak a folder, right-click it and choose Cloaking, Cloak. Cloaked folders and documents appear with a red line through them, as shown in Exhibit 7-2.

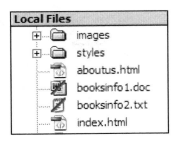

Exhibit 7-2: The Files panel, showing cloaked files

To cloak file types, right-click in the Files panel and choose Cloaking, Settings. In the Cloaking category in the Site Definition dialog box, check "Cloak files ending with" and then enter the file extensions you want to cloak.

Do it!

A-2: Checking links and cloaking files

Here's how	Here's why
1 Choose **Site**, **Check Links Sitewide**	The Link Checker panel appears at the bottom of the document window.
Observe the results	A single broken link appears in the list. In this case, a spelling error in the file name breaks the link.
2 Under Broken Links, click **locatoins.html**	You'll correct the misspelling of the file name.
Type **locations.html**	To enter the correct file name for the linked file.
Press (↵ ENTER)	The file no longer appears in the Broken Links list.
3 From the Show list, select **External Links**	To view the external links in this site's pages. These links don't indicate errors; they're listed for reference only.
4 From the Show list, select **Orphaned Files**	Several files appear that aren't linked to any pages in the site. You'll remove the image files. However, because you might need the text files later, you'll cloak those specific file types.
5 In the Files panel, expand the images folder	
Delete spice_of_month.jpg and spicebg.jpg	Select each file and press Delete.
Collapse the images subfolder	
6 Right-click in the Files panel and choose **Cloaking**, **Settings...**	To open the Site Definition dialog box.
7 Check **Cloak files ending with**	
8 Edit the box to read **.doc .txt** as shown	☑ Cloak files ending with: .doc .txt │
Click **OK**	A dialog box appears, stating that the cache for the site will be re-created.
Click **OK** and observe the Files panel	The two documents now have a red line across them, indicating that they're cloaked and won't be uploaded with the rest of the site. They also won't appear in the list of orphaned files.

HTML validation

Explanation

Before you upload your site, you should also check to ensure that your code meets compliance standards. The World Wide Web Consortium (W3C) establishes coding standards. If your pages have code errors, the pages might be displayed incorrectly in certain browsers and alternative devices.

You can validate the code in certain pages or for all of the pages in a local site. To validate the code for a page, open the page and choose File, Validate, Markup. The Validation panel opens with the results listed, as shown in Exhibit 7-3. To validate the code for an entire site, click the Validate button on the left side of the panel and choose Validate Entire Current Local Site.

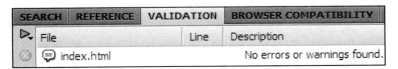

Exhibit 7-3: The Validation panel

To fix an error, double-click it in the Validation panel. The page that contains the error opens in Split view, and the offending code is highlighted. When you fix the code, that item no longer appears in the list of errors. You can find additional information about the error by clicking the More Info button on the left side of the panel.

Sometimes an error's description might not be clear, or a single code error can produce multiple similar errors. If you see this error, it's often an extra closing tag. Double-click the first instance and correct the code—you'll often find that the number of errors in the list decreases.

To find additional information about W3C guidelines, you can visit the W3C site at http://www.w3.org. You can use this site to find information about changes or additions to the current guidelines and to find specific information about certain tags, such as which ones are deprecated. (A *deprecated* tag is one that is considered outdated; its use is discouraged in favor of new elements or CSS.)

Do it!

A-3: Validating code

Here's how	Here's why
1 Open index.html	You'll validate the code for this page.
2 Choose **File**, **Validate**, **Markup**	The Validation panel opens, indicating that no errors were found.
3 Click as shown

In the Validation panel. |
Select **Validate Entire Current Local Site**	
Scroll to the top of the list	Several errors appear in aboutus.html, all around the same lines of code. When you see this kind of error, it's often an extra closing tag. Fixing the first item in the list often clears the others.
4 Double-click the first error	Split view is activated, with the code error highlighted. In this case, an extra closing table tag is causing the error.
Press DELETE	To delete the extra closing table tag.
Press CTRL + S	To save your changes in aboutus.html.
5 Validate the entire site again	All pages in the site are checked, and no errors are found.
6 In the upper-right corner of the Validation panel, click as shown	
Choose **Close Tab Group**	
7 Close all open files	

Topic B: Web site publishing

This topic covers the following Adobe ACE exam objectives for Dreamweaver CS4.

#	Objective
1.1	Describe the infrastructure required to implement and deploy Web sites.
2.3	Manage files associated with a Dreamweaver site.
3.1	Describe the methods available for connecting to a remote server.
3.2	Synchronize files.
3.3	Use get and put to transfer files.
3.4	Configure local, testing, and remote servers.

Publishing basics

Explanation

You publish a Web site by copying the site files from your local PC to a remote Web server. A *Web server* is a computer configured with Web server software and the Internet protocols required to serve pages and other resources upon request. Dreamweaver makes it easy to set publishing parameters for your site and to transfer your site files to a Web server.

A Web server is connected to the Internet via an *Internet service provider* (ISP) or a *hosting center*. The ISP or hosting center provides space for Web site files, as well as other services such as site promotion and search engine optimization.

Domain names

A *domain name* serves as both the name and address of your site. Your ISP can help you select and register a domain name.

File names

Sometimes the way you name your files can cause problems when you upload the site to a server. For example, you might upload your pages to a UNIX server, which uses different file path protocols. To create file names that comply with just about any operating system, follow these guidelines:

- Keep file names short. For ease of maintenance on the site, the file name should describe the file's content or function.
- Don't include spaces in the name. To separate words, use the underscore character; for example, *product_list.html*.
- Don't use any characters other than letters, numerals, and the underscore.
- Always start file names with a letter.
- Treat uppercase and lowercase letters as separate characters. For example, your server might not consider aboutus.html and AboutUs.html to be the same file. A good way to keep from running into problems is to use only lowercase letters.

Server connections

Before you can upload files to a Web server, you must first establish a connection between your PC and the server.

Methods for accessing a remote site

SFTP (Secure File Transfer Protocol) is a popular method of transferring files. It uses FTP, the standard file transfer protocol, and combines it with authentication and encryption protocols to protect the transmission.

WebDAV (Web-based Distributed Authoring and Versioning) is a set of extensions to the HTTP protocol that allow users to edit and manage files collaboratively on remote Web servers.

Dreamweaver can also transfer data between servers located on a LAN (local area network), and transfer data by using Microsoft technologies, such as the version control application VSS (Visual SourceSafe) and RDS (Remote Data Services).

Before setting up a server connection, check with your ISP to make sure that the Web server supports the connection protocol you want to use. If it does, the ISP typically provides information for connecting to the server. This information includes the FTP host name, the host directory, and a login name and password.

Security

When you transfer files to a remote machine, the information isn't sent directly to that machine. Instead, it's usually routed through several machines to get to its destination. Anyone along the route can access what you're sending, including your user name and password. If this information falls into the wrong hands, your account and the remote site to which you have access might no longer be secure.

Securing file transfers usually involves encrypting the files with an encryption protocol, such as the SSH (Secure Shell protocol) or SSL (Secure Socket Layer). Dreamweaver supports these protocols automatically when you connect to a server using SFTP or WebDAV.

Setting site definitions

To configure site definitions for a specific access method:

1 Choose Site, Manage Sites to open the Manage Sites dialog box.
2 Select the site you want to configure and click Edit. The Site Definition dialog box opens.
3 On the Advanced tab, under Category, select Remote Info.
4 From the Access list, select a method for connecting to the remote Web server.
5 Under Category, select Testing Server.
6 From the Server model list, select the server model used for your database connection or dynamic Web site.
7 From the Access list, select a method for connecting to the testing server.
8 Click OK to close the Site Definitions wizard.
9 Click Done to close the Manage Sites dialog box.

Do it!   **B-1:   Connecting to a server using secure FTP**

Here's how	Here's why
1 Choose **Site**, **Manage Sites...**	To open the Manage Sites dialog box. You'll explore the settings for secure FTP connection.
2 Verify that **Publishing** is selected, and click **Edit...**	The Site Definition dialog box opens. You'll explore the steps required to connect to a server through a secure FTP connection.
3 Activate the Advanced tab	If necessary.
Under Category, select **Remote Info**	To display the remote connection options.
4 From the Access list, select **FTP**	This page of the wizard is context-sensitive. When you select FTP as the remote connection type, additional fields appear.
5 In the FTP host box, enter **ftp.outlanderspices.com**	To specify the address of an FTP host where you will send files.
6 In the Host directory box, enter the path to the Test Site folder	(In the current unit folder.) The Host directory box specifies the path to the remote site.
7 In the Login box, enter your first name	For a real site, the hosting center administrator would typically assign a user name.
8 In the Password box, enter **password**	For a real site, the hosting center administrator would typically assign a password.
9 Check **Use Secure FTP (SFTP)**	

	Access: FTP
	FTP host: ftp.outlanderspices.com
	Host directory: C:\Student Data\Unit_07\Test Site
	Login: Lee Test
	Password: ●●●●●●●● ☑ Save
	☐ Use passive FTP
	☐ Use IPv6 transfer mode
	☐ Use firewall Firewall
	☑ Use Secure FTP (SFTP)

	To encrypt file transfers and guard access to your files, user names, and passwords. The Web server must be an SFTP server.
10 Click **Cancel**	To close the wizard.
Click **Done**	To close the Manage Sites dialog box.

Site publishing

Explanation

When you upload files to a Web server, the local folder on your PC (where the site resides) is automatically duplicated on the Web server. All files and subfolders are copied, except those that have cloaking applied to them. You can also publish a site to another location on your PC, either as a practice upload or because your PC is acting as the Web server.

To upload a site:

1 Define the remote site.

2 Connect to the remote site.

3 Upload a site or a folder by using the following methods:

- To upload an entire site, select the root site folder in the Files panel and then click the Put File(s) button.
- To upload a subfolder within the site, select the subfolder in the Files panel and then click the Put File(s) button.

You can also expand the Files panel to display additional options for uploading a site or a subfolder in the site. Click the Expand/Collapse button to expand the Files panel, and do either of the following:

- To upload an entire site, drag the root site folder from the Local Files pane to the Remote Site pane.
- To upload a subfolder within the site, drag the subfolder from the Local Files pane to the Remote Site pane.

Background file transfers

While your site is uploading, you can perform other non-server-related activities, such as editing pages or style sheets or generating site reports. When the transfer is complete, you can update the remote site with any changes by synchronizing it with the local site.

Synchronization

Dreamweaver synchronizes your local and remote sites by using the time stamps saved with the documents. So, if you edit and save a page on the local site, it has a more recent time stamp than the page on the server. To see which files are newer on the local site, right-click in the Files panel and choose Select, Newer Local. To see which files on the remote server are newer, choose Select, Newer Remote.

To synchronize the local and remote sites, right-click in the Files panel and choose Synchronize. You can also choose Site, Synchronize Sitewide. Dreamweaver then automatically compares the time stamps of the two sites and updates the site containing the older pages with the newer ones.

Do it!

B-2: Uploading a site

Here's how	Here's why
1 Open the Manage Sites dialog box	Choose Site, Manage Sites.
Click **Edit...**	You'll practice uploading a site by transferring the site to a folder on your PC.
Under Category, select **Remote Info**	To display the remote connection options.

2 In the Access list, select **Local/Network**

Options related to Local/Network connections are displayed.

3 Click 🗀

Navigate up one level, and open the Test Site folder

Click **Select**

To specify the Test Site folder as the remote folder. You'll simulate uploading a Web site.

4 Click **OK**

A Dreamweaver dialog box appears, stating that a site cache will be created.

Click **OK**

Click **Done**

To close the Manage Sites dialog box.

5 In the Files panel, click 🗗

The Expand/Collapse button.

6 Click ▤

(The Site Files button is at the top of the window.) To view the files in the remote folder and the files in the local folder.

Click ↻

(The Refresh button.) To refresh the panel and display the remote folder. Because there's nothing in the folder yet, only the folder icon is visible.

7 In the Local Files pane, select the root folder

(The Site – Publishing folder.) You'll upload the entire site.

8 Click ⬆

(The Put File(s) button.) To upload the site files from the local folder to the remote folder. A dialog box appears, asking if you're sure you want to put the entire site.

Click **OK**

To put (upload) the entire site to the remote folder.

Observe the folders in both panes

Both panes contain the same folders and files, except for the files you cloaked earlier.

9 Click 🗗

(The Expand/Collapse button.) To collapse the Files panel.

Site updating

Explanation
When you edit the content or design of a particular page, you can update that specific file on the Web server. Before updating a specific file, you might want to perform a *get:* download the version of the file that's currently on the Web server.

To get files from a Web server:

1 Connect to the remote site.
2 Download files or folders by using the following methods:

- To download an entire site, select the root site folder in the Files panel and then click the Get File(s) button.
- To download a specific file, select the file in the Files panel and then click the Get File(s) button.

In addition, you can expand the Files panel to display more options for downloading a site or a specific file. Click the Expand/Collapse button to expand the Files panel; then do either of the following:

- To download an entire site, drag the root site folder from the Remote Files pane to the Local Site pane.
- To download a specific file from the site, drag the file from the Remote Files pane to the Local Site pane.

To put (upload) a specific file, select that file and click the Put Files(s) button, or drag the file to the Remote Files pane.

Dependent files

When you get or put a file, Dreamweaver can prompt you to include that file's dependent files. *Dependent files* include assets and other files, such as images or style sheets, that are referenced by the file being put and that might have been altered or updated.

To enable or disable prompting, choose Edit, Preferences. Under Category, select Site. Check or clear the Dependent files options, depending on your preference.

Do it!

B-3: Discussing site updates

Questions and answers

1 What's a get?

2 What's a put?

3 How does Dreamweaver help you manage assets and files?

4 How do you enable or disable dependent-file prompting?

5 What does the Synchronize command achieve?

Unit summary: Publishing

Topic A
In this topic, you learned how to **perform several checks** on a completed site. You learned how to check the file size and download times for your pages, and how to check for and fix broken links and orphaned files. Then, you learned how to **validate your code** and fix errors.

Topic B
In this topic, you learned the basics of **Web site publishing** with Dreamweaver. You learned how to connect to a server using SFTP, and you learned how to upload a site to a local or remote folder. Finally, you learned how to **synchronize** the local and remote versions of a site, and **update a site** by transferring one or more files with a **get** or a **put** command.

Independent practice activity

In this activity, you'll define a Web site, check for broken links and orphaned files, and practice uploading a Web site by uploading it to a local folder.

1 Define a new Web site named **Publishing Practice**, using the Practice folder (in the current unit folder).

2 Check the links in the site. (*Hint*: In the Files panel, right-click the site and choose Check Links, Entire Local Site.)

3 Repair the broken link that was caused by a typographic error.

4 Delete the orphaned files.

5 Establish a connection to the Test Site folder (in the Practice folder).

   To do so, choose Site, Manage Sites. Click Edit. In the Remote Info category, choose Local/Network. Navigate to the Test Site folder and click OK.

6 View both the local files and the remote Test Site folder.

   In the Files panel, click the Expand/Collapse button and, if necessary, click the Site Files button to view the local folder and the remote folder.

7 Upload the entire site to the remote folder. (*Hint:* In the Local Files pane, select the root folder and click the Put File(s) button.)

8 Collapse the Files panel, and close Dreamweaver.

Review questions

1 On the Advanced tab in the Site Definition dialog box, what does the Case-sensitive links option do?

   A Ensures that your links work on a UNIX server.

   B Configures Dreamweaver to produce a warning box when you link to files whose names use uppercase letters.

   C Requires the names of linked files to include at least one uppercase letter.

   D Requires the names of linked files to consist of only lowercase letters.

2 How can you change the connection speed with which Dreamweaver calculates download time?

   A Select a new connection speed from the Page size/download time list in the status bar.

   B Right-click the Page size/download time list in the status bar and choose a new connection speed.

   C Open the Page Properties dialog box, select the Title/Encoding category, and select a new connection speed from the Connection speed list.

   D Open the Preferences dialog box, select the Status Bar category, and select a new connection speed from the Connection speed list.

3 How can you check links site-wide? [Choose all that apply.]

   A Press Ctrl+F8.

   B Right-click the Files panel and choose Check Links, Entire Local Site.

   C Choose Site, Check Links Sitewide.

   D Select a file in the Files panel, and click Check Links Sitewide in the Properties panel.

4 How can you cloak specific file types?

   A In the Files panel, right-click a file that you want to cloak and choose Cloak File Type.

   B Open the Preferences dialog box and select the File Types/Editors category. Check "Cloak files ending with" and enter the file extensions you want to cloak.

   C Right-click the Files panel and choose Cloaking, Settings. In the Cloaking category, check "Cloak files ending with" and enter the file extensions you want to cloak.

   D Choose Site, Advanced, Cloak files ending with. In the dialog box, enter the file extensions you want to cloak.

5 How can you validate the code for a page?

   A Choose File, Validate, Markup.

   B Choose Site, Check Links Sitewide.

   C In the Files panel, right-click the file and choose Check Page, Validate Markup.

   D Switch to Code View and choose Commands, Clean Up XHTML.

6   Which of the following are important guidelines to consider when you're naming site files? [Choose all that apply.]

A   Keep file names as short and meaningful as possible.

B   Start file names with a number.

C   Start file names with a letter.

D   Don't include spaces in the file names.

E   Don't use special characters other than the underscore.

F   Separate words in the file names with one space only.

7   Which of the following are ways you can connect to a server? [Choose all that apply.]

A   FTP

B   SFTP

C   XML

D   WebDAV

8   Which encryption protocols does Dreamweaver support? [Choose all that apply.]

A   AOL

B   SOL

C   SSL

D   SSH

9   How can you synchronize the local and remote sites? [Choose all that apply.]

A   Choose Site, Synchronize.

B   In the Files panel, click the Refresh button.

C   Choose File, Check Page, Check Accessibility.

D   Right-click in the Files panel and choose Synchronize.

10   After you connect to a remote server, how can you upload an individual file? [Choose all that apply.]

A   Select the file in the Files panel and click the Put File(s) button.

B   In the Files panel, select the folder containing the file and click the Put File(s) button.

C   Expand the Files panel, and drag the folder containing the file from the Local Files pane to the Remote Site pane.

D   Expand the Files panel, and drag the file from the Local Files pane to the Remote Site pane.

Appendix A

ACE exam objectives map

This appendix provides the following information:

A ACE exam objectives for Dreamweaver CS4 with references to corresponding coverage in ILT Series courseware.

Topic A: ACE exam objectives

Explanation

The following table lists the Adobe Certified Expert (ACE) exam objectives for Dreamweaver CS4 and indicates where each objective is covered in conceptual explanations, hands-on activities, or both.

#	Objective	Course level	Conceptual information	Supporting activities
1.1	List and describe the infrastructure required to implement and deploy Web sites.	Basic	Unit 7, Topic B	
1.2	Given a scenario, explain the requirements for supporting video, PDF documents, and SWF.	Advanced	Unit 6, Topic A	
1.3	Explain how to mitigate page weight.	Basic	Unit 3, Topic A	
			Unit 3, Topic B	B-1
1.4	Given a scenario, describe the infrastructure required to support application servers.	Advanced	Unit 7, Topic A	
1.5	List and describe the differences between client-side and server-side scripting.	Advanced	Unit 4, Topic A	
			Unit 4, Topic B	
			Unit 7, Topic A	
1.6	Describe techniques for making pages accessible.	Basic	Unit 1, Topic C	C-3
			Unit 4, Topic A	A-1
			Unit 5, Topic B	B-1
			Unit 6, Topic A	A-2, A-3
		Advanced	Unit 3, Topic A	A-4
			Unit 3, Topic B	B-2
			Unit 4, Topic A	A-1
			Unit 5, Topic A	A-1
			Unit 6, Topic A	A-1, A-2
2.1	Given a scenario, create a site.	Basic	Unit 2, Topic A	A-1
2.2	Locate files associated with a Dreamweaver site.	Basic	Unit 1, Topic B	B-1
			Unit 2, Topic A	A-1
		Advanced	Unit 2, Topic A	A-1
2.3	Manage files associated with a Dreamweaver site.	Basic	Unit 1, Topic A	
			Unit 2, Topic A	A-1
			Unit 7, Topic A	A-2
			Unit 7, Topic B	B-3
3.1	List and describe the methods available for connecting to a remote server.	Basic	Unit 7, Topic B	

#	Objective	Course level	Conceptual information	Supporting activities
3.2	Synchronize files.	Basic	Unit 7, Topic B	B-3
3.3	Use get and put to transfer files.	Basic	Unit 7, Topic B	B-2, B-3
3.4	Configure local, testing, and remote servers.	Basic	Unit 2, Topic A	A-1
			Unit 7, Topic B	B-1, B-2
3.5	Use check-in and check-out to track and manage files.	Advanced	Unit 8, Topic A	A-1
4.1	Describe options available for positioning objects.	Basic	Unit 4, Topic A	A-2
		Advanced	Unit 5, Topic A	
4.2	Design a page by using a tracing image.	Basic	Unit 6, Topic B	
4.3	Given a visual aid, explain the purpose of and/or when to use that visual aid.	Basic	Unit 1, Topic B	B-1
			Unit 4, Topic A	A-1
4.4	Work with the Properties panel and the Quick Tag Editor.	Basic	Unit 1, Topic B	B-3
			Unit 4, Topic B	B-1, B-2
			Unit 4, Topic C	C-1, C-2
4.5	Explain the benefits of using Live View.	Advanced	Unit 3, Topic C	C-1
			Unit 4, Topic A	A-1
5.1	Configure preferences for Code view.	Basic	Unit 1, Topic D	
5.2	Manage code by using Code view.	Basic	Unit 1, Topic D	D-1
		Advanced	Unit 2, Topic A	A-3
5.3	Explain how to get information about tags.	Basic	Unit 1, Topic B	B-3
			Unit 1, Topic D	D-1
5.4	Find and replace code in Code view.	Basic	Unit 2, Topic C	C-1
5.5	Explain how to select blocks of code in Code view.	Basic	Unit 1, Topic D	D-1
6.1	Create editable regions in templates.	Advanced	Unit 2, Topic C	C-1
6.2	Apply a template to a page.	Advanced	Unit 2, Topic C	C-4
6.3	Create and use template variables.	Advanced	Unit 2, Topic C	
6.4	Create and use editable attributes.	Advanced	Unit 2, Topic C	C-2, C-3
6.5	Explain the process of and issues associated with distributing template changes to pages.	Advanced	Unit 2, Topic C	
6.6	Create and use library items.	Advanced	Unit 2, Topic A	A-1, A-2
7.1	Manage assets by using the Assets panel.	Basic	Unit 2, Topic A	A-1
		Advanced	Unit 2, Topic A	A-1

#	Objective	Course level	Conceptual information	Supporting activities
7.2	Given a media type, insert and deploy that media type into a page.	Basic	Unit 1, Topic C	C-3
		Advanced	Unit 6, Topic A	A-1, A-2
8.1	Create and work with AP elements.	Advanced	Unit 5, Topic A	A-1
			Unit 5, Topic B	B-1, B-2, B-3
8.2	Create styles for typography and positioning by using the CSS Styles panel and the Properties panel.	Basic	Unit 3, Topic B	B-3
		Advanced	Unit 1, Topic B	B-5
8.3	Describe the Box model.	Advanced	Unit 1, Topic B	B-4, B-5
8.4	Create style sheets and attach them to pages.	Basic	Unit 3, Topic B	B-2
		Advanced	Unit 1, Topic B	B-2
8.5	Explain the behavior of inheritance with respect to styles and style sheets.	Basic	Unit 3, Topic B	B-3
		Advanced	Unit 1, Topic A	A-1
9.1	Validate that pages and sites conform to accessibility standards.	Advanced	Unit 8, Topic B	B-2
9.2	Describe the HTML reports that are available for testing.	Advanced	Unit 8, Topic B	B-2
9.3	Identify and fix broken links.	Basic	Unit 7, Topic A	A-2
10.1	Create forms and validate user input by using Spry widgets.	Advanced	Unit 3, Topic A	A-1–A-4
			Unit 3, Topic C	C-1
10.2	Describe behaviors and server behaviors.	Advanced	Unit 4, Topic B	B-1
10.3	Describe the role of an application server.	Advanced	Unit 7, Topic A	

Course summary

This summary contains information to help
you bring the course to a successful
conclusion. Using this information, you'll be
able to:

A Use the summary text to reinforce what
you've learned in class.

B Determine the next courses in this series, if
any, as well as any other resources that
might help you continue to learn about
Dreamweaver CS4.

Topic A: Course summary

Use the following summary text to reinforce what you've learned in class.

Unit summaries

Unit 1

In this unit, you learned the basics of the Internet and HTML. You identified components of the **Dreamweaver interface** and you learned how to customize your workspace. You performed basic Web page editing by adding and formatting **text** and **images**, and you previewed a page in a browser. Finally, you learned about **HTML tags**, including basic structural tags, and you performed basic tasks in Code view.

Unit 2

In this unit, you learned basic concepts for **planning a Web site**. You defined a Web site and you learned how to work with the **Files panel** and the **Assets panel**. Then you created Web pages, imported text from external documents, set **page properties**, inserted special characters, and used **Find and Replace** to update content.

Unit 3

In this unit, you learned how to define a basic **page structure** and how to create and modify **lists**. You also learned how to create and attach **CSS style sheets**, define element styles, and create and apply class styles.

Unit 4

In this unit, you learned how to create and format **tables** and nested tables, insert rows and columns, and set row and column properties. You also applied **fixed** and **variable widths**, and you modified cell borders and cell padding.

Unit 5

In this unit, you created **links** to other pages and resources, and you created named anchors and e-mail links. Then you created an **image map** and drew hotspots by using various shape tools. Finally, you learned about the four **link states** and you applied CSS styles to each state.

Unit 6

In this unit, you learned about the GIF, JPEG, and PNG **image file formats**. You learned about the advantages and disadvantages of using **image-based text**, and you learned how to write effective alternate text depending on various circumstances. Finally, you learned how to insert and modify **background images**.

Unit 7

In this unit, you learned how to perform **site checks** before publishing a site. You learned how to check the file size and download times for site pages, and how to find and fix broken links or orphaned files. Then you learned how to **cloak files** and **validate code**. Lastly, you learned how to **connect to a remote server** and **upload** and update a site.

Topic B: Continued learning after class

It's impossible to learn to use any software effectively in a single day. To get the most out of this class, you should begin working with Dreamweaver CS4 to perform real tasks as soon as possible. We also offer resources for continued learning.

Next courses in this series

This is the first course in this series. The next course in this series is:

- *Dreamweaver CS4: Advanced, ACE Edition*

Other resources

For more information, visit www.axzopress.com.

Dreamweaver CS4 Basic

Quick reference

Button	Shortcut keys	Function
▽	CTRL + TAB	Expands the Properties panel.
I	CTRL + I	Makes the selected text italic.
🌐	**F12**	Previews the current page in a browser.
Split		Splits the document window into Code view and Design view.
Code		Switches to Code view.
Design		Switches to Design view.
📁		Opens a dialog box where you can browse to a folder.
↗		Expands and collapses the Files panel.
⊞		Expands a tree in the Files panel.
🔗		Attaches an external style sheet to the current page.
All		Displays all style-sheet files in the CSS Styles panel.
✎		Opens a style definition (from the CSS Styles panel) for editing.
⊞	CTRL + ALT + T	Inserts an HTML table.
B	CTRL + B	Makes the selected text bold.
↻	F5	Refreshes the view in the Files panel.

Button	Shortcut keys	Function
⚓	`CTRL` + `ALT` + `A`	Inserts a named anchor.
▱		Draws a rectangular or square hotspot on an image.
▽		Draws a polygon hotspot on an image.
⬆	`CTRL` + `SHIFT` + `U`	Uploads site files from the local folder to a remote folder.
⬇	`CTRL` + `SHIFT` + `D`	Downloads files from a remote folder to your local folder.

Glossary

Assets
The components of your Web site, such as images and multimedia files.

Cell padding
The amount of space between a cell border and the cell content.

Class styles
CSS styles that allow you to give elements names that are relevant to your document structure. You can apply class styles to multiple elements on a page.

Definition list
An HTML list used for structuring terms and their corresponding definitions. Often used for glossaries, pages of frequently asked questions (FAQs), and similar contexts.

Deprecated tags
Tags that have been superseded by newer methods. For example, the `<font>` tag in older versions of HTML is now deprecated in favor of CSS.

Element styles
CSS styles that define the formatting of HTML elements, such as headings and paragraphs. An element style overrides any default formatting for an HTML element.

External links
Links to a page or resource outside a Web site.

External style sheet
A text file that is saved with a .css extension and that contains style rules that define how various HTML elements are displayed.

Font set
A group of similar typefaces that help ensure consistent text display in a variety of browsers and operating systems.

GIF
An image file format that can support a maximum of 256 colors. GIF files are best used for images with relatively few colors and with areas of flat color, such as line drawings, logos, and illustrations.

HTML
Hypertext Markup Language, the standard markup language on the Web. HTML consists of *tags* that define the basic structure of a Web page.

ID styles
Styles that allow you to create and name your own elements. An ID style can be applied to only one element per page.

Image map
An image that contains multiple clickable regions called *hotspots*.

Internal links
Links to pages or resources within a Web site.

Internal style sheet
One or more style rules embedded in the head section of an HTML document. Styles in an internal style sheet affect elements only in that document.

Internet
A vast array of networks that belong to universities, businesses, organizations, governments, and individuals all over the world.

JPEG
An image file format that supports more than 16 million colors. JPEG is best used for photographs and images that have many subtle color shadings.

Link states
The four states, or conditions, that a link can be in: link, hover, active, and visited.

Margin
The space between page content and the edge of the browser window, or the space between individual elements.

Monospaced font
A typeface in which every character uses the same amount of space. For example, an "i" and an "m" take up the same amount of space on a line. Monospaced fonts, such as Courier, resemble typewriter text.

Named anchor
A feature that enables you to mark any spot on a page as a target and then link to that target. Named anchors are also called *bookmark links* or *intra-document links*.

Nested list
A list that's inside another list.

Nested table
A table that's inserted in the cell of another table.

Non-breaking space

A special HTML character that inserts a single space without breaking a line.

Ordered list

An HTML list structure that automatically appends sequential labels to each list item. By default, list items are numbered 1, 2, 3, and so on.

Orphaned files

Files that reside in your site folders but aren't linked to by any pages.

PNG

An image file format that combines some of the best features of JPEG and GIF. The PNG format supports more than 16 million colors and supports many levels of transparency. However, many older browsers don't fully support the PNG format.

Sans-serif font

A typeface whose characters don't have serifs (flourishes or ornaments at the ends of the strokes that make up the letters).

Serif font

A typeface whose characters have serifs (flourishes or ornaments at the ends of the strokes that make up the letters).

Table cell

The intersection of a row and a column in a table. You insert content into table cells.

Unordered list

An HTML list structure that automatically appends bullets to each list item. Use this kind of list when the list items aren't sequential and don't need to be in any particular order.

Visual aids

Page icons, symbols, or borders that are visible only in Dreamweaver. You can turn certain visual aids on and off to make it easier to work with the page.

XHTML

Extensible Hypertext Markup Language, a strict version of HTML that doesn't allow proprietary tags or attributes. Instead, all style information is controlled by CSS. XHTML allows for cleaner, more efficient code. By default, Dreamweaver CS3 builds Web pages with XHTML code.

Index

A

Accessibility issues, 6-6
Alternate text, 1-23, 5-8, 6-6
AP Elements panel, 1-13
Assets panel, 1-13, 2-6

B

Background colors
  For pages, 2-15
  For rows, columns, and cells, 4-13
Background images, 6-9
Browsers, adding to Preview list, 1-25

C

Cells
  Changing width of, 4-13
  Padding vs. spacing, 4-18
  Selecting, 4-10
Class styles, 3-11
  Creating, 3-22
Cloaking, 7-4
Coding toolbar, 1-28
Colors
  Background, 2-15
  Setting default for text, 2-16
  Specifying for rows, columns, and cells, 4-13
Columns
  Fixed vs. variable width, 4-15
  Inserting, 4-13
  Selecting, 4-11
Connection methods, 7-10
CSS styles
  Creating, 3-13
  Creating, element, 3-18
  For link states, 5-12
  Inheritance, 3-19
  Overview of, 3-10
  Types of, 3-11
CSS Styles panel, 1-13, 3-13, 3-18

D

Definition lists, 3-6
Div elements, 3-11
Document toolbar, 1-8
Documents
  Basic structure of, 1-26
  Cascading, 1-9
  Views of, 1-27

Zooming in and out, 1-9
Domain names, 7-9
Download times, 7-2
Dynamic content, 2-4

E

Element styles, 3-11
  Creating, 3-18
E-mail links, 5-6
Encryption protocols, 7-10
Extensible Hypertext Markup Language (XHTML), 1-2

F

Files
  Cloaking, 7-4
  Creating, 1-6
  Dependent, 7-14
  Getting from Web server, 7-14
  Guidelines for naming, 7-9
  Orphaned, 7-4
  Putting (uploading), 7-14
  Storing, 2-4
Files panel, 1-8, 1-13
Find and Replace, 2-20
Font sets, 3-17

G

Getting files, 7-14
GIF format, 6-2

H

Heading levels, 3-2
Hexadecimal notation, 2-16
Home page, 1-2
Hotspots, 5-8
HTML, 1-2
  Tags, 1-26
  Validating, 7-7
Hyperlinks, 1-2

I

ID styles, 3-11
Image maps, 5-8
Images
  Attributes, 6-6
  Background, 6-9
  File formats, 6-2
  Inserting, 1-23